SIGHT UNSEEN

Sight Unseen

GENDER AND RACE THROUGH
BLIND EYES

Ellyn Kaschak

 COLUMBIA UNIVERSITY PRESS   NEW YORK

COLUMBIA UNIVERSITY PRESS
Publishers Since 1893
New York   Chichester, West Sussex

cup.columbia.edu

Library of Congress Cataloging-in-Publication Data

Kaschak, Ellyn, 1943–
  Sight unseen: gender and race through blind eyes / Ellyn Kaschak.
    pages cm
  Includes index.
  ISBN 978-0-231-17290-5 (cloth: alk. paper) — ISBN 978-0-231-53953-1 (e-book)
  1. Discrimination. 2. Blind. 3. Blindness—Social aspects. 4. Racism.
5. Sex differences (Psychology) I. Title.
  HM821.K38 2015
  305—dc23

                                                      2014038071

Columbia University Press books are printed on permanent
and durable acid-free paper.
This book is printed on paper with recycled content.
Printed in the United States of America

Cover design: Catherine Casalino

References to Web sites (URLs) were accurate at the time of writing.
Neither the author nor Columbia University Press is responsible for URLs that
may have expired or changed since the manuscript was prepared.

FOR ALL THE BLIND PEOPLE,
THOSE WHO KNOW THAT THEY CANNOT SEE
AND THOSE WHO DO NOT

CONTENTS

CHAPTER ELEVEN

ACKNOWLEDGMENTS

I BEGAN THIS WORK IN the late 1990s. I like to think that I would have finished and published it before the turn of the century had not the fates intervened. I was stricken with a life-threatening illness that demanded almost all my attention for many years. I did survive, but I wrote only intermittently on manageable projects. I had to keep my hand in just in case . . . or because it is so fundamentally what I do. I promised myself that if I survived I would go on with my writing and with the publication of this book. I have kept that promise to myself. And, of course, to all the blind women and men who so generously let me into their lives along the way. The stories I tell in this book represent them in varying degrees and are a compilation of the hundreds of stories I have been privileged to hear. As I have carefully maintained confidentiality and altered any identifying aspects, I will not thank any blind person by name. I am grateful to them all and hope I have repaid my debt, in part, with this book. And, of course, I thank the many student assistants who are long since successful professionals and academics in their own right.

I cannot ever thank adequately those who played a part in my very survival. They cast a wide net when I feared crashing to earth and ultimately kept me from that fate. They are my international community of colleagues, friends, and family. I want to name a few who played a special role, including Shevy Healey, Jan Faulkner, Kayla Wiener, Marny Hall, and my sister, Cheryl Uram. Also I am indebted to two gifted and generous healers, Momma Delores Lucas and Dr. Jennifer Lucas, related only through me. I want to acknowledge, in more ways than I can say with words, the sine qua non, my dear friend and purveyor of lemonade, Arlene Kock, and, finally, mi hermana del corazón y compañera de la vida, Sara Sharratt.

Any book is a group effort and represented in these pages along with me and the blind are those who read and commented on the several incarnations of this manuscript and encouraged me to continue when I faltered, especially Natalie Porter and Oliva Espin. Jacobo Schifter, Jean Maracek, Marsha Haller, and Esther Rothblum also commented on the manuscript in various incarnations. Finally, you would not be reading this book without Jennifer Perillo's belief in the importance of the project or the detailed attention of her assistant, Stephen Wesley, the production and manuscript editor, Susan Pensak, and also JoAnn Miller.

SIGHT UNSEEN

1

The Eye of the Beholder

The real voyage of discovery consists not in seeking new landscapes but in having new eyes.

—MARCEL PROUST

WE CONTEMPORARY CITIZENS OF THE planet live in an increasingly visually based and even voyeuristic world, depending more than ever on our eyes to provide information, communication, sexual stimulation, entertainment, and pleasure of all sorts. There is no way to deny that we are rapidly becoming more and more dependent on our ubiquitous visual prosthetic devices, no longer including only television and film, but computer screens, increasingly smarter smart phones, Google glasses, and all the other newly emerging "personal devices." Are we actually evolving into a species ever more dependent on visual information and communication and less aware of this evolving focus?

There are many questions to be asked and answered about the eye, what and how it sees. My questions are the questions of the psychologist that I am, one who has by now spent a lifetime trying to understand the workings of the human mind, of which the eye is an important part.

In that quest, I have studied the effects of human vision on everything from the arts (Urano 2010; De Lauretis 2010) to the social sciences (Johnston 2009; Kaschak 2013), from gender to race (Katz 2003; Katz and Kofkin 1997; Hirschfeld 2008) to sexual orientation. I have pondered the fact that our eyes compel us to face forward every time a driver in front of me and a long line of other cars politely stops for someone in front of him while I, directly behind, am not asked to consent to the delay. I have been fascinated by the way a good film tricks our human brains into believing, hopefully temporarily, that the story is real and we are all participants. How it is possible to manipulate the human mind into falling in love with a group of pixels, a manufactured image? Yet it has been done over and over again. We are all similarly susceptible to having a character in a film reach in through our eyes and grab our hearts.

As a psychologist teaching and training therapists for several decades now, I am equally fascinated by the movie playing in each of our heads and on no particular screen. Each of us is the director and star of our own personal drama. What can possibly be the evolutionary function of a faculty that leads us astray as often as it guides us? Even in one of its simplest functions, allowing us to "picture" someone before meeting her, why is it so often wrong? I have searched in many ways, informing myself through introspection, psychotherapy, scientific literature and fiction, neurology and Buddhism. I have practiced mindfulness meditation for over thirty years, and this has also led me to observe the inner workings of the human mind, most particularly my own.

Finally, travel has done for me what it does for many travelers, demanding that we see with new eyes by removing the blinders of custom so that everything becomes new and fresh as we see with beginner's eyes and mind. One day a new question occurred to me. It came into view only after a lot of thinking about the objectifying gaze that makes appearance so crucial and, in doing so, creates all sorts of adolescent miseries and maladies, many of which continue throughout life, especially for women. It came to me after publishing *Engendered Lives: A New Psychology of Women's Experience* (Kaschak 1993), which considers in depth the effects on women and men of what I have called "the indeterminate masculine or cultural gaze." My work is as much about epistemology and phenomenology as it is about psychology and psychotherapy, as much about neurology as Buddhism. And it is as much about you and me as it is about the blind people that you and I will meet together in these pages.

No answer can be any better than the questions asked, for the answers are already embedded in those questions. So I tried to formulate my questions with care and consciousness. My first question was "What if the defining sense of vision were absent?" This question has been approached by renowned filmmakers and novelists, some blind themselves (Saramago 1997), as well as by social scientists (Obasogie 2010; Friedman 2011, 2012). Freud arbitrarily took the oedipal trilogy as a metaphor for child sexuality among males (Freud, Strachey, and Gay 1989) and ignored the experience of Oedipus's sister/daughter, Antigone. In *Engendered Lives* I have tried to understand her situation as emblematic of that for many women. Freud, a man of his times, ignored the plight of the daughter and the effects of the human eye and blindness to instead focus on the cultural and personal meanings of the penis. As I am a woman of my times, I ask instead about that daughter. Considering vision, as I have done in much of my writing, I asked the next questions. "Are such crucial human characteristics as gender and ethnicity, race and sexual orientation discoveries or inventions of a species dependent on sight? How would we categorize each other, how would we discriminate were it not for the details of vision transmitted to our human brains?"

This dependence on the visual is strongly reflected and reinforced by the English language itself, which often equates seeing with knowing. Try speaking without any sight-based verbs for a day in order to "see what I mean." I have done it and I know how tongue-tied I became when I could not speak the language of sight.

Like most sighted individuals, I had never known a blind person nor had I really thought about what their lives were like. Certainly I had seen more than a few walking with white canes or guide dogs, attempting the simple, yet daunting task of crossing a city street well before the introduction of the chirping auditory aids that I have since been told are disorienting rather than useful. I have had the regular impulse to help, but also the ordinary fear of being intrusive or insensitive and so chose to err in the seemingly safer direction of doing nothing. Aside from offering assistance or serving as an impediment, I never thought of being a friend. It just did not seem possible to intermingle two such different worlds. And, honestly, it might have been just a little too frightening for me to get too close to their world.

Although I am severely nearsighted and have worn glasses since third grade, with them I can see quite well. Without them, I can readily approximate legal blindness. The world becomes a vertiginous kaleidoscope of bleeding colors and amorphous shapes. Still it does appear to me and my condition scarcely approximates complete blindness, especially given that taken-for-granted technology known as corrective lenses, my indispensable glasses.

I wanted to see with new eyes myself, to leave behind my own taken-for-granted beliefs and biases. My intention was to learn about the role vision plays in the most ordinary experiences and reactions of sighted individuals in an increasingly sight-dependent society. The part that vision plays in ordinary life has always been central for the human species; it is the way we are all designed, but nature's design requires an alchemical mixture with experience. Neither participant is of much use without the other.

During the critical period of early childhood, the lines and colors that the eyes begin to see form themselves into shapes and images that can be recognized and that take on the familiarity of meaning. The human brain, at this early age, is malleable and the most plastic that it ever will be, designed for receptivity to experience, including learning not only how to see, but what to see (Quartz and Sejnowski 1997; Edelman and Tononi 2000). So is the human heart still in formative stages and, if the truth be told, so is every cell in the human body.

Once this period of neural plasticity comes to an end, somewhere close to puberty, both vision and language become impossible to learn. Having not learned any language at all, the child is deprived of this skill for a lifetime. Having not learned vision, she will never be able to see more than a disconnected and incoherent set of lines and shapes. Even a second language learned after this same critical age will always be spoken with the accent of the already learned language (Bialystock 2001; Flege, Yeni-Komshiam, and Liu 1999; MacKay, Flege, and Imai 2006).

Visual development must be early and must be orderly. A group of lines turns into a staircase, another into a mother's face or a father's comforting arms. The familiar sight of mother perhaps comes to mean home, that of father safety. Or they can signal danger. There is no therapeutic approach in the world that has shown much effect in altering these deep meanings, for they are introduced so deeply by the eye to the heart and mind where they intermingle freely with their other inhabitants. In concert, they all will recognize and respond to these sights for a lifetime and in an instant.

Absent this sequence of development, the result is chaos, a staircase or a door a jumble of lines and colors, even the planes of a mother's face nothing more. As a result, individuals whose sight has been restored in adulthood through some innovative form of surgery can not master the learned skill of vision and are generally overwhelmed, the putative blessing of sight turning into a curse. These individuals rarely see any relationship between objects that they have learned to recognize by touch and the mélange of lines and colors that bombard their newly opened eyes. Because humans develop familiarity with faces and facial expressions at specific times in our lives, those who are deprived of human contact or changing facial expressions at that age often have trouble reading expressions for their entire lives. Formerly blind people are often face-blind or unable to decipher emotion from facial expression. Some have trouble differentiating between male and female faces (Inglis-Arkell 2013). Eventually virtually every one of them has chosen to close his eyes to the fragmented and chaotic sight that can never become vision and to return to the comfort of the familiar world based for them in the prior act of touch.

There is even more startling alchemy involved in what we call normal sight, the well-functioning eye/brain duet. Every human eye has a blind spot near the center of the visual field. This is not about peripheral vision or a view from the margins. It is right at the center of experience. The eye does not know its own blind spot, mistakes it for vision. Nor does the mind's eye.

Every human brain fills in what is missing, blinding each of us to our own blind spot (Durgin, Tripathy, and Levi 1995). A human paradox, each of us sees where we cannot and do not. The mind is positive that it sees what is really there. The arrogance of the human mind, of the human eye is rooted firmly in physiology. Of this personal vision, a worldview is born and an entire life lived. Yet the center does not hold because it does not even exist. Right in the middle of each person's universe is a big dark chasm into which each of us must inevitably tumble again and again unnoticed and unnoticing.

Nor is this the end to the acrobatics of the human eye. The eye presents its offerings to the brain upside down. From this occluded and inverted presentation, each brain creates a unitary vision, a single image, and turns that image on its head, a full 180 degrees, setting each of us back on firm ground. Each team of eyes and brain collaborates with light to produce a world set right, seemingly solid and safe, one in which it is possible to take a stand. For this firm ground to wind up under our feet rather than hanging above us depends upon the finest tuning, the closest relationship among all the participants in this visual project. Firm reality makes this pact with the visual trickster.

The eye is both guide and trickster; vision and trompe l'oeil intermarried simultaneously inform and perform their tricks, reaffirming their eternal vow. Human sight, progeny of this marriage, is born naive and must be educated, must be socialized. Every eye must not only learn how to see, but what to see and how to "make sense" of the sensory fragments it is presented. As nature nurtures and educates her young, a collection of lines becomes a staircase, another a balloon, another a flower or tree. A group of shapes emerges from surrounding shapes and one day becomes a particular house, a place forever to be recalled as home. A group of lines on a page becomes an alphabet and a word and a whole new world emerges.

Neonatal vision peeks through a window of opportunity, a window that, if not opened frequently when it is new and pliable, soon becomes rigidly and permanently sealed shut and opaquely curtained. Not seeing in time, the human eye will never be able to focus at all, the mind to create sight. The eye remains unmoved by recognition, the mind by possibility. "The cubic centimeter of chance" is lost (Castaneda 1998).

It is an irreversible golden opportunity, as meaning combines with light, time with the eyes and brain, movement with blindness to produce vision. Those lines will never again be less than a group of words, those surfaces and planes a face. The time when lines were not letters, letters not words, surfaces not yet a face cannot be recaptured. There is nothing but to face forward, eyes ahead.

This same human eye can forever after recognize these patterns where they are and fill them in where they are not, each time as much an act of creation as of recognition. And the human heart is also part of this equation. It not only recognizes these sights but also comes to delight in them, anticipate them or even long for them. Life forms itself within and around these patterns.

And in another act of magic, of human alchemy, the brain and DNA encode copy after copy of all these sights and store them whole and in fragments in the mind/heart, store them in every cell (Pert 1997). These are living copies that wait impatiently, that throb with life as they inhabit an inner landscape, as alive and lush as any jungle or forest. And like the forest and the jungle, they are part of an ecology of other sights and words, feelings and memories. Nothing and no one is ever alone. Experience engraves itself not just as history but also as an internal geography. This inner landscape is composed of memory and desire. And it begins in the eye of the beholder.

Since I will rely on my own vision in this book, let me use an experience of mine as an illustration. I divide my time between California and Costa

Rica, the two San Josés that have come to define so much of my life. When I first visited the jungles of Costa Rica decades ago, my friends excitedly pointed out to me the monkeys in the trees. They were all around us, everywhere, hundreds of them, but I could not see a single one. A native of New York City, I could spot a mugger or a taxi blocks away, but a monkey in the trees, never. My eyes were not trained to this sight. It took practice, learning first to distinguish the patterns of greenery from each other, until I began to see little faces embedded in them everywhere. And once I saw them, I could never go back, could not unsee them. It is a sight that my brain/heart and not just my eyes now inevitably recognize. In a similar way, the eyes of the psychologist or the biologist, the astronomer or the archeologist are trained to see what each discipline defines as its monkeys. Even more important, each of us constructs a life, a worldview out of what is possible for us to see and names it reality when it is instead only possibility. Were the monkeys more or less real as I began to see them?

Vision then is a learned skill much like speaking, like language itself. We might do well to consider sight a language, so imbued is it with meaning and nuance. Wherever the eye rests, the mind enters. And, once it does, what is seen is melded seamlessly with what cannot be seen in this inescapable form of visual and conceptual alchemy. In this act of perpetual creation and recreation, perspective is born. The most seemingly simple and objective act of sight, from the first moment, contains pattern and thus story. Every moment of sight is also one of vision.

There is more to this story. The glue that holds together this seemingly sensory exercise of perception is not simply material. If it is material at all, it is the material organized by nonmaterial psychological and energetic fields that encompass matter. It is the mattering that educates the naive eye and turns it able to perceive sights that matter that allowed my eyes to see the monkeys in the trees.

In fact, the stuff of which images are made is the stuff of meaning, or what I prefer to call mattering, which encompasses both mind and heart, meaning and caring. Mattering defies the fragmentation of human experience so dear to contemporary psychology with its separation of thought and feeling, cognition and affect, mind and body. It contains and organizes matter, but is not limited to it or by it (Kaschak 1993, 2013).

Mattering is the name of the gravitational force that holds us all to each other as much as the Newtonian/Einsteinian kind of gravity holds us each

to the planet. It is the glue for biology and neurology, psychology and sociology, physics and anthropology. It is the glue of a life lived among and
with other people. The very images that begin to form in the eye of a small
child are based not only in neurological or biological development. Both of
these are, at the very same time, a social act and, thus, an experience of mattering. Social context guides the formation of vision, much as it determines
not only the development of language, but of which language develops and
becomes the mother tongue. The human brain is ready for the task, deliv-
ered complete with the architectural scaffolding of verbal and visual grammar (Chomsky and Ronat 1998; Bailey et al. 1994).

In the first moments of contact with another person, each of us ven-
tures a myriad of guesses and judgments about that person (Unger 2006).
Undoubtedly this unconscious split-second reaction once was and still may
sometimes be necessary for survival itself. It is not difficult to grasp why
it is so crucial for each person to be able to assess any stranger as friend or
foe, safe or dangerous, potential sexual partner or not. Each of us develops
a facility with a culturally and personally intermingled code that instantly
informs us in any encounter of some combination of gender and age, race
or ethnicity, class and sexual orientation, health, attractiveness, and more.
While it is possible to become reasonably aware of these judgments, it is
probably not within human capacity to transcend or eliminate them in
adulthood, as they are already embedded in our brains, eyes, and hearts and
encoded in every cell.

In the twenty-first century the role of vision has far transcended the intimate local interpersonal. Technologically based means of visual extension
and prosthesis have themselves become more and more ordinary and ubiquitous in the early years of this century. Sophisticated camera equipment
is in the hands of every cell phone user. The images captured in this way
as well as others can almost instantly be sent around the planet to those
with the equipment to receive them. Scientists can almost as easily watch
the brain in action with the prosthetic aid of functional MRIs and PET
scans. Among other perhaps unintended consequences, the popularly available equipment has wrought havoc with earlier notions of privacy and
will require a more relevant development of many ethical principles upon
which cultures, systems of justice, and even health care have relied. Techno-
logical eyes are everywhere that biological ones cannot be.

I began to wonder, in a society without sight, how would the judgments and perspectives developed visually be made. In fact, would ideas so visually based, such as those about attractiveness, gender, or race have ever been invented? Since I could not find that society to study and I was after something closer to consensual reality than to fiction, I settled on the next best thing, individuals in my own hypervisual American society who had never had access to sight. Obviously anyone who has had sight, even briefly, would have had access to these and a multitude of other personally and socially constructed experiences that so define the prevalent viewpoints in American and other Western societies.

What better place then to begin my paradoxical nonsightseeing journey than with those who do not have access to vision? I wanted to find out how they fared in a world so rooted in sight. I do not mean that I was interested in what is named disability per se, in how they were able to cross the street at a busy intersection, but how they survived in a culture where interpersonal systems of knowledge are so embedded in vision. Did they develop an entirely different system, a different first language, and, if so, what was it and how did it stand up to the language of vision? These were my earliest relatively unformed questions. I wanted to learn what I could about sight by staring into blind eyes.

This project then was something of a vision quest with at least two preconceived purposes. The first was to find out what it is like to be blind. The second was to find out what it is like to be sighted, or what I came to think of as normal or ordinary blindness.

As twenty-first-century sciences now acknowledge, we are all interrelated and interconnected in many ways that are not just visual or based in the acknowledged five senses in which scientific empiricism cloaks itself. In fact, the moment you approach someone, or perhaps even think about her, that person is influenced and so are you. This principle has been shown to be the case even in studies of single cell organisms. It is impossible not to influence even such an organism, much less another human being. This observer effect, first formulated by Heisenberg (1925) is being applied more and more by prescient thinkers in all areas of knowledge. I myself will not then abide by the rules of reductionist empiricism, which would lead to the common pretense that my influence can be controlled, but will instead try to expose it in all its detailed finery.

I will do this by trying to make my vision, the eyes of the beholder, as much a part of the story as what I see as I try to put together pieces of a gigantic puzzle, a puzzle whose pieces add up to a different perspective. Not one of those puzzles where mountains, sky, and trees slowly emerge to the recognition of the vigilant eye trained to recognize landscape. And not even the faces of monkeys peering out at me from the jungle foliage. This is a puzzle that none of us has seen before, that no one can see. It has no views or vistas. There is nothing to be seen. It is a world without sight, the world of the blind.

As we begin, we are exploring what can be thought of as a mattering map (Kaschak 2013). Every person's mattering map is a work in progress and is never static as long as that person breathes life. For some, it is slow moving and would require an earthquake to alter the terrain. For others change is more frequently and more readily achieved. I mean this map to replace the more static and linear ideas of what is often named personality by my own profession or what have come to be touted as gender, ethnic, and other human differences naively reduced to a snapshot. I mean to erase the arbitrary boundary that reductionist science draws around the individual, separating her from all that is named context. We are also learning from twenty-first-century physicists and biologists and ancient Eastern ideas that what the Western eye sees as space is far from empty and is also part of the complex metaphorical map of life (Lipton 2006a, b).

The maps of individuals intersect and overlap more or less in each case and at each moment in time. For example, two people who are well attuned to each other would have, for much of the time, overlapping mattering maps. A rebellious adolescent would have a map different from his parents and the larger culture, but probably similar to a particular subculture with which he identifies. And color matters. I do not mean by this to refer to the pinks and blues that are used on world maps to signify different countries, but instead the color of human skin that is still used to define and categorize us all.

Such a map does not contain artificial boundaries such as the imaginary line between society and personal experience. Much like the boundary between the United States and Mexico, these separations are material illusions, imaginary lines that are imbued with the human meaning that make them real enough to die for. Yet they are built on shifting sands. This living, breathing map also moves and morphs in response to every imagined or actual contact and in response to every aspect of context, from the personal to the cultural. In other words, it is as alive as is each person, each group, and each culture.

This idea of mapping is compatible with what we are currently learning about neurology, the functioning of the human brain. Such investigators as Gerald Edelman and his colleagues (Edelman and Tononi 2000) are using scanning equipment to peer into the brain at work and at play. What they are discovering and inventing, because their own vision is already carefully trained and based in what concepts the human mind can achieve, are overlapping brain maps, mattering maps themselves. Let us see if the human idea of multiple maps is a useful one in this circumstance.

You, the reader, are invited on this adventure with me. I begin with the questions, most of which grew out of my experiences with blind people. I do not yet, at the beginning, know any of the answers. As a result, you may see me stumble over my questions again and again. I will not try to make my awkwardness invisible to you. I will also not tell you how things turn out, except as they do. I invite you instead to come along with me. Because you are with me, you too are changing the story, really are part of the story. I will be as mindful as possible of your position right beside me and will try to be as hospitable as possible to you, to remember that when I stumble you may also, especially if you are leaning heavily on me.

At the start, I thought I was like an anthropologist studying a tribe isolated from modern culture. I did not see the satellite dishes on the roofs of their huts. But I am getting ahead of myself. Starting with those who have never had access to the learning process that creates vision, I hope to unravel some of the mysteries of a visually based culture such as that of the twenty-first-century West before it covers the entire planet, fueled by the spread of American-based technology and consumerism.

Since I am a therapist as well as a researcher, I knew the importance of time and trust in developing relationships that allow certain confidences and observations. The more this study developed, the more it became apparent to me that it would take time and commitment on my part and on that of every blind person who kindly agreed to participate.

I began by generating, with a group of graduate students, a series of questions that we thought would elucidate these matters. The students, ten in number, eight females and two males, two African American women, one Latina and one Latino, five white women and one white man, then each worked with one or two blind individuals in a structured interview format. They were to offer some sort of assistance to these blind individuals so that the exchange was as equal as possible. This included taking them shopping and other activities with which the blind person requested assistance. We tried to achieve parity and, in this way, not exploit them as traditional research subjects. Eventually I met hundreds of other blind individuals and have woven many of their stories into the composites that emerge in this book. You will meet these blind participants in each chapter and will learn who they are in much greater depth and detail. Of course, many of the particulars are changed in order to protect their privacy.

I have never considered self-reported conclusions very useful, as they offer only what is in the immediate awareness of the respondents and what they are willing to disclose to a stranger. I was looking for something much more complex, contextual, and possibly not available to awareness, something I had to undertake myself, as these students could not be expected to accomplish these goals. I was not yet sure that I could either. I was not yet aware that the blind are not a community as the deaf often are and that getting to know several of them would require patience, endurance, and the better part of a decade.

As you read this book, you will come to know each blind person and you will come to know me. I will make visible to you my own ideas and reactions and my own mistakes. Someone else might have said and done other things in these situations, but I acknowledge by my methods that I am not someone else. I spent hours with these blind people. I tried not to be intrusive, but rather involved, maintaining an attitude of mindfulness gleaned from some forty years as a clinician and almost as many as a practitioner of mindfulness meditation. I brought along a tape recorder, as I am well aware of the unreliability of memory. When I could not tape, I took extensive notes. Thus my students were able to continue in the role of transcribing and I continued to benefit from their enthusiastic discussions. They were, of course, instructed to transcribe every word, sound, and pause. It is I who have, by my own hand, made them presentable to the reader. It is I who also disguised these narratives so that they are not recognizable as individuals.

As I consider language of paramount importance, I try to reproduce conversations as accurately as possible. As human communication is so nuanced and complex, I also try to convey that complexity. There are quotations only where I consider it important to maintain exactitude.

Otherwise the words have been made more accessible to the reader. This also means that I respectfully use language to maintain more complex and nonreducible ideas. I did not yet know when I began how important the idea of translation would become. Nevertheless, I have chosen to retain the voices of the participants and my own: in that way empowering the reader to add yet another perspective.

The conversations I have reproduced here have been edited for the reader's eye. I could say that I simply transferred the spoken to the written language, but that would be disingenuous. I have taken the liberty of doing the editing and so I am implicated also in the shapes and meanings that emerge. Yet I am not alone, as you the reader must see through your own eyes, along with mine and with blind ones.

Although I have tried to report these conversations in a much more transparent manner than is the convention of my own profession, I can only fail at this enterprise just as I begin, every word simultaneously revealing and concealing. None of these discussions is simply a conversation between two people, although they all are that. Each of the conversations in this book is haunted by the specter of vision. The sighted culture is everywhere with its flirtatious engendering and seductive racializing ways, teasing us into believing momentarily that we can step outside and observe its effects, whereas we are deeply embedded inside them and they inside each of us. The paradoxical complexity of these simple conversations should not be lost on anyone. Yet I have tried to live inside this paradox, to keep my eyes and my mind both educated and naive in the best senses of both words.

I am a participant in these conversations, but I am the participant who gets to formulate and ask most of the questions. These people were gracious enough to invite me into their lives. While I have become closer to some of them, none insisted, none questioned or broke the implicit rules of the interview. As much as I tried for mutuality, I cannot trick myself or the reader into the illusion that I achieved it. What I can do is try to make myself as visible as each blind person. In this fieldwork I am as much a part of the field as any of them. I propose to accomplish this not so much by analysis or commentary as by invitation. I invite you to come along with me to these interviews, for that is literally what they are.

Are they any more than stories? We live in a time when those who are designated to tell the truth do not and when the very disciplines that search for truth declare it dead. It is replaced by mnemonics, by story, by a psychologically based relativity. The boundary between truth and fiction is everywhere and, at the same time, nowhere. One of the early questions that I had was whether there is indeed any territory to explore or are there only hauntings and illusions. I asked the question, "Is there a border between the seen and the unseen worlds? If so, can I slip across unnoticed and unseen?" Perhaps we will discover the answer together.

I have tried to give some degree of transparency to our conversations by not reducing them to taxonomies, by not taking the life out of them by categorizing or labeling them. I have also tried to maintain the tension between literalness and abstraction that I hope will represent subjectively and correctly what I set out to accomplish. While I took along my own psychological compass, there were no maps to guide me. I feared that maps of adjacent territory would only trick me into thinking that I already knew where I was going and how to get there. Finally, I have tried to write with the fullness of respect for the complex lives of those who invited me in or at least did not turn me away when I knocked on their doors. The tension of their individual uniqueness and their commonalities is also one that I have tried to maintain. If there are times when I do not succeed at this endeavor, it is more for lack of skill than of intention.

Any story is told by a storyteller, and here I am that storyteller. Although the blind participants created these stories with me, they also told them for me. I can never know how they would have told them to another listener or another questioner. I came armed with my questions, but only in the most general sense. I wanted to follow where they led, but I do not delude myself into the belief that I only followed. The questions are mine, although the answers are not. Yet the questions shape the answers, just as my lifelong eyes shape the telling and the seeing. My goal was transparency, but if I had achieved it you would see nothing.

Let me tell you as much as I can right now about where you find yourself. You are located within the territory of narrative ethnography, coming into use in psychology via anthropology. This approach requires prolonged involvement in real-world multiple complex contexts (Lavis 2010; Maracek 2003) in order to understand subjective meanings and perspectives and necessarily includes a reflexive awareness of the influences of the researcher (Camic, Rhodes, and Yardley 2003). Multiple perspectives increase accuracy; however, this level of involvement also creates unanticipated ethical dilemmas, which we will encounter together (Hill, Thompson, and

Williams 1997) and solve together. The first involved a good enough disguise so that none of the participants is recognizable, and, after much consideration, I did decide on this procedure.

If you want to start with me by your side, then I am standing as a starting point before the idea/question that perception is culturally and personally developed through learning, that vision is only one epistemology or way of knowing the world. Our next step is to seek out and hopefully discover this process by locating it in those who have never had access to vision, individuals blind since birth. Although we will meet many, we will concentrate, in depth, only on a limited number, whom we will get to know well through multiple contacts (Sandelowski 1995; Griffin and Bengry-Howell 2008; Oleson 2005) over a period of several years.

I am particularly interested in perceptions of sex, gender, and race.

At the beginning I chose to maintain a flexibility in the methodology in order to be able to benefit from experience along the way (Wertz et al. 2011). Along the way, I hope that their nonvisual concepts will provide a mirror for the sighted development of these ideas.

I want to be able to observe what is embedded in ordinary interaction. My methods will develop as we proceed and as needed, just like the strategies for any journey. The focus of this work then is not to present biographies of the disabled and their plight in a sighted world. It is not even about disability. And it is not about monkeys. But it is about sight, how it is learned and how it is used. How do we come to know what we know, come to believe most what we see with our own eyes? And how do we come to base entire cultures in our own human vision? I invite you then to hitch a ride on my question.

2

Blind Date

In a dark time, the eye begins to see,
I meet my shadow in the deepening shade;
I hear my echo in the echoing woods.
    —THEODORE ROETHKE

RATHER THAN JUST IMAGINING ONE, I am about to enter a sightless universe. I hope that what I see and don't see will help answer my questions and yours. The human senses create invisibility in the very act of visibility. We relegate most of the sights and sounds all around us to the unconscious, which gives the conscious mind respite from the constant assault of sensory stimuli. Otherwise the flux of sights impinging on the human nervous system every moment would be overwhelming. If we could see the world with bumblebee eyes, we would experience an entirely different fragmented environment. We also see fragments, but other eyes see even more or different fragments. We cannot see the world with any eyes but our own, but we can travel and see for ourselves different sights and different visual distinctions. We can see, for example, how in Vietnamese markets dogs as pets and dogs as food are sold side by side. Shoppers can only tell the difference by the color of the cages. We can witness lines drawn down the middle of a foreign street denoting an international boundary. We can ponder age-old feuds between groups that, to an American eye, seem identical. Yet they can instantly recognize and threaten each other.

With these ideas in mind, I begin my relationship with Jesse. Jesse, who is in his mid-fifties, has been completely blind for more than twenty years. During that time, he has had a successful career as a social worker and psychotherapist, working mostly with troubled adolescents. When he started down that path, he could still see the road and that helped him in his studies and then in his early career. However, what Jesse saw even then was the peripheral vision of macular degeneration, literally a marginal view from which the center is missing. Unlike in ordinary blindness, this center cannot be filled by any trick of the human nervous system. It remains dark and empty.

Jesse spent most of his younger years preparing for the inevitable total blindness. Early on, he devised a plan. He would create a personal cartography, mapping his shrinking universe and memorizing these maps. Once he was completely blind, he would follow his mental maps. Every day, before or after work, he walked around a different section of his Berkeley neighborhood, carefully noticing everything he saw. He learned by heart the order of the streets and their intersections. He knew by the number of steps he took where all the cafés, restaurants, and bookstores were, and he was familiar with every part of the large campus that is the center of life in this part of Berkeley. Jesse anticipated that he would remember these landmarks later on and would be able to navigate with his carefully constructed memory map. It was an intelligent and courageous plan, and it served him well when the time came for him to depend on it.

In his mid-thirties, what Jesse had dreaded finally happened. The sights of Berkeley disappeared completely from his view. Even the slim margins he had seen were gone. He now had to learn to live as a blind man. In truth, he had already begun his education years before by using his sighted time so wisely.

I too am beginning to navigate a new world. Although my sight is relatively intact, vision is not very useful to me in confronting the challenge of seeing into a blind world. I will need, at least in the beginning, a guide and a teacher to point out the nonsights along the way, to fill in my preliminary picture of life without vision. No amount of intellectual understanding or reading can prepare me, and, in fact, I do not want to see through the eyes of others, but, as much as possible, to see for myself.

Seeing through someone else's eyes is the work of the psychologist, the researcher, and the psychotherapist that I have been for decades. I will use my fresh insights to understand the experiences of people who have no vision. I am hoping to gain a new understanding of the role of vision in the lives of those of us for whom it is a central and crucial way to make sense of the world. I want to investigate the absence of sight to learn about its presence, its uses, and its natural domination of everyday experience. It is this assumption of naturalness that I want to expose as not so natural at all, but learned so early in life as to function automatically or what my profession calls unconsciously.

I am ultimately after the blindness of the sighted.

I plan to explore the lives of women and men who have never seen at all, whose ideas, perceptions, and biases have not entered their brains through their eyes, but through a different route. I will then compare these ideas with those based on sight. Ultimately I will come to know people who have never had sight, but for now I decide to take Jesse as a guide and use his unique position between these two worlds as a starting point.

So Jesse will be my first blind date. I am eager but nervous too. What will he come to be in my life and I in his? Will I like him? Will we connect? I want him to like me and want to "see" me again. And there it is already in my language and my thoughts, the sight at the center of my mind and my words. How will it be to meet with this man who cannot see me?

Jesse is expecting my call; a mutual friend, Ethan, fixed us up after I told him about my project. Jesse answers the phone on the first ring in a warm and friendly voice, and we make plans to get together. "Meet me on Monday morning at the Café Med," he suggests. He adds a detail to his instructions: "You will recognize me by my white cane." I'm not sure if he is being wry or simply stating a fact. I decide not to navigate the shoals of irony in this alien circumstance. I simply repeat his words as if they are instructions that I want to be sure I've gotten right. "You will be the one with the white cane. I'll see you there on Monday."

Before I introduce you to Jesse, let me tell you about my preparations for our meeting. It is Monday morning, and I am getting ready the way I do for a professional appointment. I, who have spoken and written against judging women by appearance, am nevertheless caught up in my own version of this practice. The dress code is as complex as the most difficult spy code, although more easily accessible as it lives in my own body. There is so much meaning, a surplus of meaning for a woman, embedded in the choice of hairstyle and color, makeup and jewelry. Pants or skirt, suit or sweater and shirt, blue jeans or sweats? (Of course I would never wear sweats to a meeting, but jeans are a serious possibility.) Each of these items means something different on my woman's body than it would on any man's, as gender expresses itself everywhere (Kaschak 1993).

Then there is the not-so-simple matter of shoes: sneakers, heels, flats, or boots? Each choice is imbued with cultural significance subsumed under the rubric of fashion, but containing other profound meanings. Picture this woman. Is she tall or short, fat or thin? Try her now with some different hairstyles and colors, with or without glasses. Does she wear makeup, and, if so, a small subtle amount or is it visibly encrusted on her face, highlighting rather than concealing blemishes and lines? How about jewelry? Does she sport a large diamond or a thin band, long dangling earrings or a nose ring, a heavy pinky ring or a delicate filigree one? Is she wearing a dress or pants, a skirt with or without a matching suit jacket? Pantyhose or socks? Flat shoes or heels? Are her colors bright or muted, serious or frivolous? Each of these meanings, encoded in a heel or a skirt, the fabric or cut of a blouse, telegraphs competence or incompetence, traditional or progressive values, formality or friendliness, professional or casual attitude. They are all designed to convey gender, class, age, and perhaps even sexual orientation. In modern Western society, we have grown accustomed to having these matters telegraphed almost immediately and visually. At every new encounter, visually based judgments occur in a split second and often unconsciously.

As I prepare to meet Jesse, not a single item on my body is simply serviceable. Everything reveals and conceals more about me than I can know. Each of us wears our cultural composition of identities with varying degrees of habit and intention. Of course, this complex code would be too much to think about consciously every day, just as would most habitual behaviors.

Consider how much the face can signal at a glance. Skin color, the size and shape of features, often reveal race or ethnicity and are supposed to make gender instantly apparent. Research has shown that perceived attractiveness affects all manner of judgments about others in an instant. Entire bodies of literature in psychology and sociology, anthropology, and linguistics reveal what is read in faces, bodies, and the slightest physical movement. I myself have contributed to that literature and to the decoding process as well. The code can be either subtle or blatant, but is decipherable only in the complex interplay of a particular culture and the equally particular psychology of an individual living in that context. For a full reading, neither can be ignored.

I don't want to review here what I and others have already said, but instead to take another important step in deciphering these visually based codes. I cannot even begin to ignore these nonverbal messages. How would I do it? Not wear clothing? Put a bag over my head? These would speak even louder. I can choose to rebel or conform, to make a conventional statement or an outrageous one, a subtle one or a confusing one. I can choose between a great variety of statements, but I cannot opt out, cannot choose silence within the context of this cultural chatter. Or so I thought, with an innocence that I had not yet lost as I prepare for this first blind date.

I wonder how Jesse anticipates meeting me. Does he question if I am tall or short, fat or thin, black or white? Does it occur to him that I might be Asian or Jewish or Persian? Disabled in some way? Young, old, or middle aged? How will he know and what will he imagine? Will he imagine at all?

These questions occupy just a few brief seconds before I become aware of what I should have known all along if my mind and body were not so much captives of culture. Jesse will not know the difference, does not speak this language, and may not even know or remember that it is all around him. To Jesse, I have no face or body, no hair and no jewelry, unless he can touch them. Will he even imagine what I look like? Can he? We have spoken on the telephone. He has heard my voice, knows my gender, and understands my professional interests. As he once had some sight, does his mind form visual images of me as mine does of him? Will such images carry the cultural meanings of his last time of sight, the early 1980s? Will he see me the way I might have looked during that decade? Or is his own code a completely different one that is invisible to me? So many questions already.

I leave my home in Oakland for Berkeley, a brief and invigorating drive through the succulent spring greens and acacia yellows of the East Bay hills. It has rained almost nonstop this winter, and the hills are unusually lush. Today, for the first time in what seems like months, the sun is shining brightly. My spirits are immediately lifted, a gray internal haze breaking open into emotional sunshine. Although this experience is said to be chemically induced (Amasio 2008), I wonder if it is that simple. It is said to be the effect of neurotransmitters in the brain. As they are released, so am I, they from my brain cells and I from an equivalently gloomy cell in which my spirit has taken seasonal refuge.

Does Jesse even know that the sun is out today? If he does, does he know it from a weather report on the radio or do his body and spirit know it as well? Does it lighten his walk as he comes to meet me in the Café Mediterraneum? Does it make him want to whistle or hum a tune? To swing his white cane a bit more jauntily perhaps?

In a brief twenty minutes I am in Berkeley, right on Telegraph Avenue where we are to meet. I take care to park my car as close as possible to the cafe, as I will have to interrupt our discussion to feed the insatiable parking meter in just under an hour. In Berkeley this is no idle ritual, but a vigilantly monitored and serious source of revenue. In the precise choreography of collection, a ticket will appear on the windshield in one hour and one minute.

With unexpected ease, I am able to find parking right off Telegraph Avenue. I make my way through the street carnival of homeless people, some still asleep on the sidewalk, a few awake and asking for spare change, several vendors opening for the business of hawking T-shirts and jewelry in the familiar shape of peace signs. Among this street chaos, reminiscent of the London of the Middle Ages, right up to the rotting garbage in the street, a few UC Berkeley students move purposively to their classes. The rest have nowhere in particular to go.

I know the Café Med well. It is not one of the trendy eateries that have sprung up in almost every American city in recent years. No one is running an insurance business here via cell phone and iPad. No one is drinking molasses pumpkin coffee. No one is here to see or be seen. This café is quintessential 1960s Berkeley, a living time capsule. Its habitués now include homeless persons seeking the daytime warmth of a steaming coffee and a heated room, a few students and professors, and many holdovers of an earlier day who have seemingly forgotten to move on or even to cut their hair and change their clothes. The room is dark and cavernous, with crudely drawn but colorful murals on the walls and an unchanging air of musty aging bohemia. Of course, Jesse would have no way of knowing any of this—or would he?

As I enter the café, I scan the room to see if he has arrived first. No white canes as far as I can see. I look at each man in the room, holding his gaze long enough to see if he is blind, if he could be Jesse. I realize that I never walk into a café and actually look at anyone so directly. I especially do not look a man right in the eye, which would be taken as a form of invitation.

Every one of the men looks back at me, holding my gaze, invitingly curious. I avert my eyes before anything more develops, while it is still my move.

A blind man with a dog enters and I wonder if Jesse has a dog and didn't mention it. I quickly dismiss the thought. Of course this is not Jesse but another blind man. He is not the only one in town, especially a town like Berkeley, which prides itself on its hospitality to the disabled community. At the appointed time, Jesse appears (I do not, of course, appear to him) and heads directly to the counter to order his coffee. He is using a white cane, as he said he would be. He does not search me out in any way and, I suppose, expects me to find him. He is of medium height with the thinning hair of middle age. His skin is the pinkish-yellow color that society calls white. He is dressed casually in brown pants, a plaid shirt, and a gray windbreaker, and his eyes are plainly in view to me. He does not wear sunglasses. The visual impression is a muted one. It whispers to a sighted person, "There is nothing to notice here."

I approach Jesse and announce my presence. He extends his hand a few inches in a gesture that I don't recognize. It is not quite the familiar American handshake; his arm remains only a few inches from his side. Of course he cannot gauge the space between us, yet the customary handshake suddenly appears invasive and aggressive by comparison. I take Jesse's hand with an awkward unfamiliarity.

Jesse is not awkward in his response to me, but direct, warm, and confident. We spend a few minutes ordering coffee, my usual double espresso and his customary latte and croissant. I mention that I have already staked out a table, and, with the casualness of familiar custom, he asks that I lead him there. He takes my arm. In a sighted relationship this would be too soon for touch. But touch as a sign of intimacy does not apply in this situation. Jesse lives in a different time frame from mine.

He is easy and cooperative, a colleague, having once taught sociology courses at UC Berkeley. He has many ideas about blindness and about blind people and is eager to discuss them. He seems as interested in my ideas as I am and we begin to talk enthusiastically and easily. I ask him for permission to record our conversation, although the background din makes us both wonder aloud what the recorder will pick up. At least the tones and context, if not the precise content of the conversation. I am careful to place the tape recorder unobtrusively in a corner of the table. I suppose I worry that Jesse will spill something on it or knock it over. This says more about me than about him, as I immediately spill my coffee in my effort to avoid his imagined clumsiness.

Since Jesse once had some sight, he knows about eye contact and arranges himself to appear to be looking right at me. I am surprisingly captured by this visual paradox and compelled by years of custom to keep looking at the two openings on his face from which he does not see. He is aware of this and remarks proudly that this kind of eye contact makes him seem more like a sighted person; he is delighted with this trick, this ability to pass.

For my part, I find myself unable to resist this demand for eye contact that does not exist. I look directly at him for the entire first hour, transfixed. Then I excuse myself to add four more quarters to my parking tariff. On the way back, I resolve to try to defy years of socialization and networks of axons and dendrites in my brain and not look at Jesse as he speaks. With great difficulty, I am able to do so for brief times, the demands of a lifetime of custom and neurology directing my eyes more strongly than that of circumstance. The habits of conditioning rather than condition compel me to look, just as Pavlov's dogs were compelled to salivate in the absence of meat. And this is precisely what Jesse has come to count on. He and I are engaged in a performance of sorts, following a script in which he pretends to be sighted and, from careful memory, invokes my sighted responses. He has learned to live theoretically, to fake vision and to try to pass as a sighted man. He is very practiced at this deception.

It is here in the café that Jesse tells me about his early preparations for blindness, how he tried to notice everything—from the Eiffel Tower and the pyramids to all the streets of Berkeley. He describes how he set himself the task of remembering sights and landmarks, faces of friends, intersections and cafés, gathering up as many acorns as possible for the long dark winter ahead. It occurs to me that Jesse collected experiences and sights in much the same way that I did when I was young. Yet my desire for adventure and experience grew out of a need to escape the barren landscape of one of the many look-alike suburbs of 1950s America. Jesse's pursuits were more methodical—and more poignant—as he prepared for a blinded future.

He begins to tell me how he got to our meeting this morning, a very different route from mine.

"My disease was macular degeneration. It was hereditary." He continues with a description of his youth, his university years, and finally his ever approaching blindness.

"I see," I respond, as he explains about the macular degeneration that began to rob him of his sight. I hesitate to use the word *see,* but I don't know how else to express that I understood what he has just said. I'm aware of how much the sighted world equates seeing with knowing. So instead of backing away, I plunge in.

"I noticed that you said to me on the telephone, 'I'll see you in the cafe.'"

"I do that sort of on purpose a little bit."

"Do you? For what reason?"

"I don't know. I guess I just want to use the same words as everyone else, to speak the same language. I used to be able to see. I used to be a good student, at least until I had to take calculus." He doesn't smile at this half-humorous self-deprecating comment. He continues. "A blind friend of mine explained to me once that in using words like *see* you can sound like you know all about whatever is being discussed." Now I am beginning to see just a little more.It's about twenty minutes before noon.

"I don't want you to miss your train to work, but I would really like to meet with you again," I say to Jesse.

"Sure."

"Maybe I could meet some of your friends if that's possible."

"I'll ask my friend Andrea about it." Only later will Andrea herself tell me that they are a couple, and even later she will tell me that they have broken up. Jesse never mentions this, although as we get to know each other he talks about her frequently.

"That would be great," I say. "So we'll be in touch soon."

I drive Jesse to the busy intersection of the downtown Berkeley BART station. He gets out of my car and begins, with the aid of his cane, to find his way to the entrance. Instantly he is much less in control and much more vulnerable than he was in the café or than he has described himself as being. In fact, he seems disoriented and circles the BART station reaching with his cane for contact with something solid; but the cane keeps stirring the air around him. I have unintentionally dropped him a few feet away from his customary bus stop and he has memorized the steps to the BART from that spot only.

Should I get out of my car and offer help or should I respect his professed independence? No wanting him to feel ashamed or exposed, I sit silently in my car watching him circle the station a few times until he gets his bearings. I feel uncomfortable, as if I'm spying on him. But to turn away would be worse. I learn in those brief moments the difference between his confident description of his abilities and the way he actually manages to get around. I also learn something about the intrusiveness of my own vision. This is not the last touching moment Jesse and I will share.

We continued to meet once a month for about a year. Our conversations were always interesting and informative. I grew to like and respect him more and more. He eventually introduced me to Andrea, who had been blind since birth. He also invited me to visit his workplace. Yet Jesse stayed formal and professional, and I followed his lead. I could see it was his way of maintaining his sense of self. Maybe it was more comfortable for me as well. I didn't want to cross beyond the borders of collegiality either. I too can be shy and hide behind formality. We were, in that sense, made for each other.

At our next meeting at Café Med we resume our conversation. Jesse and I have both given a good deal of thought to our earlier discussion, and we begin where we left off. Or, rather, he does.

I was thinking about what you said last time about reacting to visual appearance so strongly. I was probably like other young men when I was an adolescent, noticing the appearance of women as the first and most important thing. Only later, when I lost vision, would I be paying attention to other things, the intelligence and sensitivity in someone.

"I actually had an interesting experience when I was living in Phoenix," Jesse continues. "I was becoming friendly with a woman from India. We would go out to dinner and have these big discussions about Eastern religion and things like that. Somehow, in my mind's eye, I had a picture of her like not particularly attractive, but intelligent looking."

I am all ears now.

"I found out later after she left the U.S. that she was extremely beautiful. She had even been a contestant in a Miss Universe contest. But that was an example where I would form a picture in my mind of a womanly buddy that I could go out with. I did meet her later in England and asked her about it. She said that she kind of liked knowing a blind person who didn't respond to her external features."

"I bet. It was probably a different experience for her too not just to be judged by her appearance."

Jesse has given me a gift, an anecdote that precisely illustrates one of the main points I hope to make and have discussed with him. He is right;

he is a good student. I decide to mine this vein as much as possible, proceeding cautiously.

"So if I kind of pushed you to conjure up an image of what Ethan [the male friend who introduced us] looks like, what would you say?"

"Let's see. The face is the part that would come first. He would be about medium size with brown hair perhaps, but the part in the imagery that I would notice would be a thoughtful, attentive facial expression. In his forties. I've never asked anyone what he looks like."

His assessment is almost completely wrong. The guess at size is accurate, probably based on hearing where his voice comes from. They are about the same height, two or three inches taller than I am. Ethan is also in his fifties with a full head of gray hair and a full beard, also gray. He needs reading glasses, and they're often perched on his nose. I do not say this to Jesse and give him instead that neutral "uh huh" of the therapist. I have something else in mind.

And here I go. "Now would it be too difficult if I asked you to try and describe me? I know that's putting you on the spot a little."

"No, it's all right, but I'm thinking that I would probably be affected by some of the things I know about you. Your professional background."

"Yeah. You already know quite a bit about me."

"You should wear glasses and you should be intelligent."

He is cautiously circumspect, but has given me enough of an answer. Like his Indian friend, I invoke the stereotype of an intelligent woman, the precise opposite of a beautiful one in his mind. Ethan, equally intelligent and a professional as well, does not invoke the tension of contradiction. I decide not to tell Jesse whether he is accurate or not, in case I want to pursue this later. Instead I adjust my glasses and continue.

He goes on. "When I became legally blind, I didn't want to admit the degree of my visual limitations. I learned that I could fake it a little bit. There was a feeling, a kind of shame that went along with it."

"How did you do it?"

"You know the way you remember the days of old-time radio, how you fill in the experiences? I still tend to do that."

Jesse is counting on the memories of what he once saw. He judges me by a twentieth-century stereotype in which intelligent women looked "brainy." For better or for worse, in the twenty-first century, a woman is supposed to be all things to all people and had best be beautiful as well as intelligent, sexy as well as nurturant. In a way, I long for those simpler days, although my generation of women were complicit in the change. We did not perhaps consider the Law of Unintended Consequences, for this change was not what we intended at all. We hoped not to judge and be judged by appearance, but size and shape matter perhaps more than ever. Although we may be considering piercings and tattoos in addition to heels and corsets, this is not the difference for which we hoped. And smaller is still better, perhaps even more so, for women only. Size matters, and an ever growing number of young women starve their bodies into submission.

So Jesse had retained some visual pictures of what people and places might look like. They continued to influence and reflect his ideas. I have yet to learn about the thoughts and ideas of those who had never had access to sight. That is coming next. But before we get there, I want to mention that one of my sighted graduate students inadvertently decided to contribute a piece to this puzzle. Transcribing my conversations with Jesse every week or so, she is confident that she knows what the Café Med looks like. She has heard not just our conversations but also the ambient sounds and my descriptions of the rooms. She wants to tell me how she is picturing the Café Med and is sure that she is accurate. This is what she tells me.

"You enter and on your left is a door, through which is a narrow L-shaped room. It is long and narrow." She does not know, nor do I, from what recesses of her own experience her mind has produced this image. Her mind's eye imposes sight—cannot do otherwise. It wants to see the scene and does not care if the scene it sees is the real one or not. It is the seeing that matters.

A week later I meet with this student in Berkeley and take her to see the café she has imagined all these weeks. She instantly recognizes all the sounds, the buzz of talk from the other tables, the insistent steam of the espresso machine. Yet the café itself looks nothing like the cafeé of her imagination. She is somewhat surprised, as if she had expected to be able to construct an identical Café Med in her mind. This speaks even more assuredly of the blindness built right into vision. From this incident, I developed the practice of trying to picture people and places in advance. I am more often wrong than right. When I later check with other sighted individuals, they are also more often wrong than right. I wonder about this odd and misleading function of visual imagery that both serves and fails to serve simultaneously.

Many of the confidences Jesse so generously shared with me would become themes that emerged over and over as I traveled through this new world. The idea of faking it or passing became more important as I spoke with other blind people. It would continue to express itself in other settings in all its false finery. The sense of profound shame or loss of self would prove to be related, much as Jesse suggested. I will return to these and other themes in the chapters that follow.

Here is one more story about Jesse. It is about the day that I drove him to work. He works in Fremont, at Casa Juventud, a halfway house for disturbed adolescents. "Halfway" means that they are between hospitalization and a return to life in the community. It is work that I could never do. It is slow and takes great patience. The rate of recidivism is unrelenting. Residents are much more likely to wind up back in the hospital than they are to be back in the community. For me, it is discouraging, as I tend to focus on all those who are not helped rather than the few who are. Mine is the impatience of the disappointed idealist, but Jesse is able to appreciate the work and the challenge.

On a hot Thursday afternoon in June, I drive to Jesse's apartment in Berkeley to take him to Casa Juventud. If it is hot in Berkeley, I know it will be brutal in Fremont. Although I am picking him up at his apartment, Jesse asks me to meet him outside. I want to see how he lives, but he begs off, saying that he is too messy "like most men." He evokes my interest in gender for his own purposes, and I know it will do no good to persist. There is something he doesn't want me to see. It may indeed be his messiness, but it may not. I respect his desire for privacy and for the limit he is setting. He much prefers to tell me his own version of his story than to have me see something that he has not seen first. Jesse has his pride.

When we made this date he felt it necessary to warn me that he is not a driver. Again he was not joking at all, and the poignancy of the comment struck me. I was taken aback, until I realized that he was trying to tell me that he didn't know how to get to Fremont by car. Instead he takes BART and two buses to get to work every day. I assure him that I will check a map, but I have not—for two reasons. First, I have a pretty good idea of where Casa Juventud is from his description. But, more important, I decide it will be interesting to observe how the two of us navigate together and how we discuss it—what language and landmarks each of us uses. So I thought it best not to plan too closely, but instead wait and see how things turn out. I did not anticipate what actually happened.

As I pull up to Jesse's building, two men standing out in front ask me if I am looking for "the blind man. He was out here and just went back inside," one of them tells me. I had been waiting a little further down the block by mistake. Jesse would have no way of knowing that and, in this case, neither did I. For different reasons, I did not see him and he did not see me. I wonder if Jesse is aware that these men were looking out for him. Before I have too much time to ponder this, Jesse appears.

He has something else on his mind besides the weather or these men. "I got into a hassle with the police on Sunday," he says. He tells me that a friend was coming to pick him up and double-parked in front of his building.

"Just as I came out, there was a policeman who wrote up a ticket." Jesse hardly pauses. "I didn't think they gave people a ticket for brief double-parking like that."

"It's possible in Berkeley," I say, but I've never seen them give a ticket to a blind man. That is going just a little too far."

"He was one of those very authoritarian policeman," Jesse says. "He wrote out the ticket anyway."

He had tried to talk the policeman out of it and even complained later to a sergeant, but to no avail.

"I think they make their entire revenue in Berkeley from tickets," I say. I am amazed at a system that would give a parking ticket to a blind man. I can only wonder what they might have done had he been speeding instead.

Jesse gets in the car, and I drive through the streets of Berkeley, down Ashby to the entrance to Highway 80, which, in a few exits, passes the Bay Bridge and San Francisco on the right and then connects to Highway 880, which goes almost directly to Fremont. When we have to get off the freeway in Fremont and navigate the city streets, my experiment in internal mapping begins awkwardly.

"We're getting near Fremont," I tell Jesse. "I have the address and, with a few landmarks, I think we can find it."

"I hope so," Jesse says. "Unfortunately this is part of the mapping that I don't do very well. I could ride with people a lot in Fremont and not really remember the way the streets go. But, if you see some of the streets, you can ask me about it," Jesse replies gamely.

"OK. I know where the BART station is and I'll be able to see it soon after I get off the freeway. That is a landmark for both of us, since it is where you begin walking every day."

"What street are we driving on?"

"We're on the freeway now coming up to Mowry Avenue. I'm going to get off here."

"Yes. Mowry is the turnoff."

"That's what I thought."

"At least I remember that part," Jesse remarks.

I am surprised that he feels he must participate this way. He seems nervous.

"That's one of the things I know," he goes on. "But I don't remember where to go, if it's left or right after that."

"That's not a problem. I think I can get us to the BART. You said it was not far from the BART, so let's try for that. Oops, I got off in the wrong direction."

"That's all right," Jesse assures me. I've given him a chance to save face by also making a mistake. It was not intentional; I'm picking up Jesse's nervousness and getting anxious myself.

"It feels like the car was moving at a good speed today," Jesse says.

"That's true. We are just ahead of rush hour, which starts at about three. This is part of my commute to San Jose, so I know the traffic patterns all too well from years of making this drive."

Jesse asks, "What streets do you see?"

"We're on Oliver and Mowry."

"I know that's somewhat in the vicinity of where I work."

"I think the BART is further down here. I'll be able to see the BART going above us before we get to it."

Jesse is concerned that he doesn't know how close the BART comes to the street, and I assure him I'll find it. Rather than yielding this part of the navigation to me, Jesse insists on participating. And he's obviously getting more and more nervous.

"Do you see any other streets? I know when we get close to it you'll probably have to look at a map unless we find the actual BART station."

I try to reassure him. I do know exactly where the station is, although I have no idea of the last part of the drive. I assume that Jesse does, since he walks it every day. But he is still upset, and I say, "I'll go look at a map or I'll stop and ask somebody in a gas station so I don't make you late."

"I know how to get from the actual BART station, you know, walking," Jesse reminds me.

"That's why I think that once I find the BART station, we'll be fine. Central Avenue is coming up."

"If you see, you know, big buildings or shopping centers or something like that . . . " he goes on.

I read him the name from the sign. City of Fremont Civic Center and he recognizes it.

"We're close to that."

"Good. We're at a park, and the Civic Center is here with a bridge over some water. We're going toward BART. We're in back of a tractor, so we're moving slowly." I am still trying to reassure him by giving him some of the visual information. I have continued directly toward the BART station.

"We are crossing Park Place now," I tell Jesse.

"Park Place goes parallel to the road we are looking for. We're very close. Is there a McDonalds?"

"There's a Taco Bell on the corner. Also a Bank of America and a Denny's."

How can Jesse possibly get oriented? I wonder. We could be on any suburban street corner in America. I couldn't find my way either if someone dropped me on a street corner with a Taco Bell and a Bank of America. I couldn't even tell you what city I was in.

In retrospect, I think it would have been better not to give Jesse the visual information he kept seeking, but just to reassure him. He didn't seem to think I knew what I was doing, and he could not depend on his own senses. He was caught between two worlds and not able to function well in either. Jesse did not like to be out of control. I understood.

"This is very close to Casa Juventud," Jesse opines.

"Well, now there's a gas station, so I can ask for directions. You think we should be on Mowry Avenue now—is that it?"

"Mowry goes right past the park that I was telling you about."

"Well, we are having a new adventure. What do you think?"

"It shows how my map doesn't work that well."

"It just works differently. How would you be expected to have a map of this part?"

But he does seem to expect it of himself. I fear that I am chipping away at his carefully arranged self-esteem.

I pull into a gas station and ask for directions while Jesse waits in the car. When I come out I say, "They tell me we are very close. Exactly what you said. We're very close to it, just a few blocks down and across from the McDonalds. Exactly what you were saying. Your map is not bad."

I am walking a tightrope now, trying to support his esteem while gathering the information I need. It's not easy to maintain my balance, but at least I don't fall off. Jesse rebounds.

"Well, I was just picking out a couple of highlights. For the route I know best of all we don't even need the BART station."

We have found the McDonalds near Casa Juventud. Jesse appears to feel much better, and I have learned something about how his internal map works or does not, just as he has said. I have also learned about the concentration and repetition that it takes for Jesse to feel safely in control of himself. Are he and I that different?

"We're passing the park on our left now," I tell him.

"OK. Just about when you get to the BART tracks, you turn left."

"Here come the tracks. Now I turn left?"

"Yes."

"Uh-oh. I'm on a one-way street. What did I do wrong? OK. We are on Eleventh Street."

"OK. Then we're going to the edge of the park. You turn left again."

"What am I looking for, Thirteenth Street?"

"Don't look for that. Just turn left." Jesse is becoming impatient, and he's trying even harder to direct my driving without the information I need. I feel his anger. But I am not being stubborn. I just cannot do it his way any more than he can do it mine; I cannot drive the wrong way down one-way streets.

"Here is H Street. We're at Eleventh and H. There's no left here."

"Maybe I don't know about left turns and right turns and all that kind of thing," Jesse responds. He seems annoyed. "So now there's a youth center in the park. And we're right across."

"We're at Eleventh and G."

The names of the streets are irrelevant in Jesse's world. "Forget about that. I don't know about that," he says impatiently. We are both growing frustrated with the differences in our maps. He is insisting that I follow his lead and will not let me find my own way. He will not yield and does not trust my map at all. And I cannot drive on his kinesthetic one, ignoring one-way streets and stop signs.

Finally we pull up outside Casa Juventud.

"OK," I tell Jesse. "I'm going into the parking lot now. OK?"

"I guess you can park here," he says hesitantly.

"Yes, it's a parking lot. Maybe I could come in with you for a few minutes?" I ask. I'm sure he is as exhausted and frustrated as I am with this last part of our journey, but I ask anyway.

"Sure."

"I don't want to intrude," I say. I feel we have both been through enough for one day and I'm also concerned about the confidentiality of the residents, who have not agreed to meet with me.

Casa Juventud is a big, slightly run-down old house. When we go inside, I see that it's filled with old furniture and has the musty smell of a place that hasn't been cleaned or hasn't had any fresh air in a long time. I have been in these residential placements enough to recognize the smell. Jesse's job is at the bottom of a hierarchy of mental health positions, but it is a job, and Jesse does it with pride and dedication. I stay only briefly and leave before any of the residents return. I am sure he still needs to recompose himself, as I know I do. I am not going to get to see, at least on this day, how he works with people. Later on he will describe some of the difficulties, telling me that he works best with a cotherapist who can see, for example, if one of the group members has gone to sleep or is annoying another, breaking the carefully defined rules of behavior so essential in this kind of placement.

Jesse shows me around the facility.

"As you can see, the residents are out." He continues to make frequent reference to what I can see.

"They are at school or a day program or something like that. There's a recovery group for people with drug and alcohol problems tomorrow. There's a business meeting. There are also some of the kinds of groups that are similar to the sort you'd have in a mental hospital. Saturday we have outings. I used to be one of the outing counselors. That was an interesting way for me to get to various things."

Jesse looks reflective. "Sometimes I feel like being blind gives me a spe-cial rapport," he tells me.

"They see me as someone who also has something wrong. I might be more aware of the way things impinge upon somebody who has a disability. You know, whether it's the stereotypes or whatever, some of the residents feel a kindredness with me. I've also noticed—I don't know if this is really so—but I think with certain kinds of mental illness, like paranoia, people may feel a little bit more comfortable with somebody they don't think is scrutinizing them too much."

"You're safer for them in some ways," I acknowledge.

"I don't look at them, so they don't have to be hypervigilant with me. So in some situations it works for me not to be able to see." Jesse continues to tell me about his job.

"I have two or three resident people that I work with on an individual basis, that I'm officially assigned to, but the roles in a halfway house are more informal, and sometimes you might get into informal counseling. Or sometimes one of the things that happens is that residents will, in a friendly way, offer to walk with me across to BART. I can actually get there OK, but that leads to more informal conversations."

Jesse has now returned to familiar territory and is back in control. Direct-ing the conversation makes him more comfortable. His nervousness—and mine—subside.

I say good-bye to Jesse and stroll over to the park to rest and get my visual bearings. The process of translating from a visual language to a kin-esthetic one and back has exhausted me. I am almost dizzy with disorienta-tion. In contrast to the run-down 1960s house that is Casa Juventud, the park is very well cared for and attractive, with brightly painted slides and sandboxes. It's about 2:00 o'clock, and the park is empty. I find the first bench and collapse on it with gratitude for its very presence.

A BART train passes almost directly overhead. I glance around. The houses around the park are all rundown California bungalows, typical of working-class neighborhoods, although even these neighborhoods are becoming gentrified as the price of real estate climbs. The houses are in vari-ous states of disrepair, just the sort of area where a halfway house can coex-ist without any complaints from the neighbors. The street is barren and dusty, with a few lonely saplings trying bravely to survive. Next to my car is the ubiquitous shopping cart of twenty-first-century America. It is empty at the moment, but there is undoubtedly a homeless person attached to it. A police car cruises idly by.

A huge vintage 1960s red car with three Latino young men sitting almost too low to be seen also cruises by slowly in a cultural reflection of the police car. Across the street, an old beat-up American car is parked, perhaps permanently. Someone could be living in it. Soon I notice a school bus coming slowly down the street. With school out, there will probably begin to be more activity in the park and on the streets. Soon enough, the streets start to fill with teenagers carrying books and backpacks. They are lively and energetic, talking loudly to each other and to invisible companions at the other end of their cell phone connections.

As I return to my car and head toward the freeway, I think how much easier it is just to drive out and see Mowry Road in front of me and the BART station above me and be able to orient myself visually. It is the relief of not having to translate, decode, or have my eyes serve someone else. I can relax and let the visual messages go straight from my eyes to my brain; they have been trained as a team. I am surprised at how exhausting this experience has been for me. Jesse's impatience made it all the more so.

Jesse wanted to pass, to appear to sighted people to be sighted himself or at least able to maneuver as well as a sighted person. Although his control strategies could be viewed as gendered, gender was not what shouted the loudest at me. Instead it was the poignancy of trying to compensate for the enormous loss he had suffered. The eye contact. The street directions. The more he tried to demonstrate that he had not lost too much and was prepared for it, the more I saw how he had organized his life around the unimaginable loss he suffered in his youth. And the shame of it, as if it were his own fault, as if he had to work constantly not to be perceived as a lesser person, a lesser man. His was an ongoing struggle to gain or feign control, and it was a gendered struggle, for how could it not be? He was a man, wasn't he?

The sighted world and the English language equate seeing with knowing, and I began to realize how much I am a product of that equation. At this point I experienced myself the enormous effort at translation of sighted language as well as the not so intentional representations of the sighted codes built right into vision. Jesse's understandings of gender, of racial and ethnic differences, his map of Berkeley and the rest of the Bay Area, were all rooted in his prior sight and remained historic rather than contemporary.

But he had accommodated. In fact, he had told me that he and his blind friends understood that it is possible to "use words to sound like you know all about whatever is being discussed." That is precisely what Jesse did with me, and quite successfully. He gave me lucid examples of his ability to pass, although I did not yet think of it in these terms.

What he was doing was practicing an art that would soon become familiar to me. He was "passing" in much the way a gay person, a light-skinned black person, or some Jews have tried to do, loss always being embedded in the dubious gain of this strategy. Of course, his performance was not as seamless as that of others, but it was still very much a performance. He proved this to me in many ways, including his assessment of my appearance based on his gender stereotypes. He performed gender for me in that way and in the distress that he could not hide while riding in my car. In doing so, he illustrated just how much of a performance gender is.

On the car ride I forced the issue of our contrasting maps as the differences began to appear to me. Clearly Jesse was already an expert in the matter while I was a novice. Soon I would learn more about the tremendous price he had paid and I would learn more about the price that I and other sighted people pay for citizenship in our world.

Jesse and I met many more times. He continued to be very helpful in answering my questions and introducing me to blind friends of his. His fingerprints are on all the stories in this book. Jesse had opened the door to the world of the blind for me, and now I was ready to enter it more fully by myself. The rest of my time would be spent with people who had been blind since birth, men and women who had never known what Jesse had learned in those few years in which he still had sight.

3

The Color of Blindness

No object is mysterious.
The mystery is your eye.
—ELIZABETH BOWEN

SOMEWHERE ALONG THE EDUCATIONAL WAY, most Western students are introduced to the poetry of Homer, the *Iliad* and the *Odyssey*, and taught that he was a blind man. This myth is meant to induce awe that he could be blind and so accomplished. I would not want to be a blind student in those classes. I'm sure I would feel that I had something enormous to prove. Attending school in the late 1950s and early 1960s, I know that I felt this way because of my gender. My aspirations were not considered appropriate for a girl, even one who could see reasonably well with her glasses.

According to historical fact, Homer was probably not even one man, but a composite of unnamed authors who contributed to the development of these cultural epics. What is the evidence that he or any of them were blind? Since the use of colors in the texts does not match our current usage in complexity or hue, linguists have debated whether they were written by a blind man who was fudging these descriptions or whether instead the Greeks of the period named colors differently or even saw them differently, whether the cones in the retina that permit color vision at certain wavelengths were less developed in these ancient Greeks (Gladstone 1858).

Isabel has inherited this Western concern with color indirectly from our culture and directly from her mother, who is interested in art, architecture, and interior design. Isabel is also what contemporary Western society, here again influenced by these same Greeks, names a lesbian. She is in her late twenties and completely out about her sexual orientation, while trying in whatever ways she can to conceal her blindness.

As I came to learn more about blindness, I understood why Isabel would want to take on such an epic challenge of her own. It is really an impossible goal, but impossibility does not deter Isabel. She is strong and smart and a quick study. She perfects her skills through constant practice, and I must admit that it took me a while to understand what she was doing. Once I did, I tried to help her, as I too am no stranger to the impossible task and can take it as a challenge. To me the words *impossible task* sound like an invitation, and I suspect that they did to Isabel as well.

Isabel did not have Jesse's temporary opportunity to see, and so her ideas about the sighted world are based entirely on hearsay, description, and explanation. Not surprisingly, she has a lot to say about sexual orientation and gender and about not just being a lesbian but making sure that she is seen as one. As we get to know each other, we discuss what this means to her and what it means to me. She and I also explore the meanings and experience of color in a variety of contexts, including the colors of human skin, on which Western perception has placed so much importance for so many centuries. These are all crucial issues for Isabel, as they are for most of us. But I am getting ahead of myself. First I want you to meet her much as I did.

I began to talk to friends about this book at the lunches and dinners over which we meet. This is the twenty-first-century adult replacement for the corner candy store of my New York childhood. In speeded-up American daily life, many of us are too busy to prepare a meal at home or to head spontaneously to the corner after supper. Public meals, sandwiched between appointments, are instead the preferred community ritual. It is a very old-fashioned form of multitasking. At these meetings, we catch up, consult with each other, and discuss our new projects, books, and sometimes lovers. I am as enthusiastic about the idea for this book as I used to be about a new romance. Several of my friends know blind people, and they offer to fix me up with them. My blind dates unfold more easily than my few unnerving experiences with the more traditional kind, which have been for the most part much less successful.

I meet Isabel in this very way. A mutual friend gave me her name. "You will really like her. You must talk to her." It turns out that she was right: I do like her as I come to know her and as we become friends.

Again I make that first phone call, the one in which we are still on equal footing, both blind to each other and listening as closely as we can to vocal cues. Isabel responds with enthusiasm. We make an appointment for the following Wednesday at eleven. She lives on a hilly San Francisco street right off Bush Street in the Fillmore District. The area is centered around a busy Fillmore Street, with its shops and cafés, slowly changing over from hippie to yuppie, from stores selling incense and Jimmy Hendrix posters to upscale restaurants and expensive boutiques offering Italian shoes and designer clothing. Only the large organic food market and the taste for healthy food survive this cultural transformation.

In this first conversation, Isabel says she could just as easily come to the East Bay to meet with me. Just as easily? I wonder why she makes this offer so casually. If I were doing someone a favor, as she is doing me, I would not offer to spend an extra hour traveling. So is she a more generous person than I am? If I were blind, I certainly would not offer to navigate a trip to another city to be interviewed. Or would I have something to prove? I also wonder whether there has been some mistake and she is not actually blind. I myself have been temporarily blinded by this offer. Only later will I come to understand that this is precisely its purpose, along with Isabel's conviction that she can cross the bay just as well as I can. She is probably right. I am definitely wrong.

Nevertheless, I insist that I come to her. She suggests an early morning time, one that would make the Bay Bridge rush hour traffic a serious impediment. When I mention this, Isabel pauses for a long moment, digesting the information carefully. It had apparently not occurred to her, or else she did not know about traffic on the bridge. She does not reveal which it is, in fact does not comment at all. Of course she is blind. I have so much to learn.

Checking her schedule again, Isabel notices that she has a free hour at eleven on Wednesday, and we agree to meet then. She gives me detailed instructions about how to get to her house. Coming off the bridge, take 101 to the Fell Street exit, followed by a few familiar lefts and rights. At the end of the instructions, which she must have given many times, she mentions that I will be able to recognize her house as it is painted red. Again I wonder if she is actually blind. She is trying to speak the sighted language, much as Jesse had, but with less visual basis, as she has been blind all her life. Jesse was, in a certain way and to a certain extent, bilingual and was the first to help me understand the degree to which visual language is embedded within ordinary expression. Isabel would continue to enact it for me, trying whenever possible to speak my sighted language. Frankly I had been hoping to learn to speak hers.

This is my second blind date, so I have some idea, albeit still quite unformed, of what to expect. I did not have to concern myself with my image. For the first time in my life, I had no image. What would that be like? For one thing, I could be a professional woman without the intense effort that goes into looking like one. I did not have to struggle to create an image of a competent and intelligent woman, combining strength and soft-ness, assuredness and understanding, toughness and nurturance. I will not convey these qualities with my clothing or shoes, my jewelry or makeup. No visual message will be telegraphed announcing my arrival on the scene.

I easily follow Isabel's instructions, but when I get to her house I discover it is not red at all, but white. The house next door is red. I am momentarily confused. Do I have the wrong address? I check my address book one more time, but it confirms to me that her house is the white one. I wonder who told Isabel that her house is red, and why? Did she misunderstand or was someone playing a cruel joke? How many other people has she instructed proudly with this piece of misinformation? Obviously no one has mentioned it to her. Nor do I. Isabel is trying to pass in the sighted world, much as Jesse did. She speaks sighted language, but she can never know from her own experience if she speaks it correctly or not. She must depend on other people's eyes to help her communicate with yet other people's eyes. I can only imagine the vulnerability of her position.

I climb the long flight of San Francisco stairs to her house and ring the doorbell. The names are written in the letters of the alphabet familiar to sighted Americans and right underneath in American Braille, which I can-not read. After what feels like a very long time, Isabel comes to the door. We introduce ourselves, and she holds out her hand, keeping her upper arm next to her body in a gesture almost identical to Jesse's, again making me aware of how the customary gesture involves flinging a hand across the space that divides two people. More than that space divides Isabel and me right now.

Like Jesse, she suggests a café for our meeting. We readily agree to walk the three blocks to her favorite one at the end of Fillmore Street. Everyone in San Francisco and Berkeley seems to have a favorite café. (I am writing in mine right now.) I wait for a few minutes while she readies herself and searches for her white cane. It is in plain view for me and I am confronted again by the same question. Do I tell her or not? Is it presumptuous to tell her or not to tell her? After a short time of watching her fumble around, I decide to tell her where the cane is. The other way felt too unkind, and common sense won out, but I am left to wonder about the suitability of a sense that is not actually common to Isabel and me.

With my eyes, I can take in Isabel's entire appearance in just a few seconds. She is a little taller than I am, her face freckled and her blonde hair cut short and straight. Her smile is easy and friendly. She appears to be at least ten years younger than I am, maybe more. Later she will confirm that she is indeed precisely ten years younger. She will also explain to me that she asked her sighted roommate to cut her hair in a "lesbian style," so that other lesbians would be able to recognize her. She didn't know what they saw, but wanted them to see it in her. It is an interesting and creative strategy. Her hair is short and streaked with highlights, but is it a lesbian hairstyle? I am left to ponder this question. Is there even such a thing as a lesbian hairstyle, at least away from a context of other cues and behaviors such as dress and movement? And what if a heterosexual woman has all these characteristics? What would that mean? I have more questions than answers at this point.

Isabel's solution to this complex problem is simple but entirely understandable. She counts not only on the obvious fact that people who are sighted see something that she does not, but also that they can help her duplicate this sensory information. Can she make sense out of nonsense, even with the help of her well-intentioned friends? As I consider the possibility of signaling "I am a lesbian," I imagine from inside my own vision that the signs are multiple and must be read in context. Even then, they can be misunderstood. In fact, Isabel's hairstyle does not shout "lesbian" at me, but I will make a point of finding out how well this "signal" has worked for her.

We begin the walk to Fillmore Street. Isabel takes my arm instead of using her cane. She can orient herself more easily by my movements than by using an inert stick. It is the easiest way for her to walk beside me, but much too soon for physical contact in an ordinary sighted meeting, especially for this particular sighted person. I do not comment or refuse her, but I do feel a certain discomfort, a sense of being trapped in instant intimacy. Our relationship will clearly not be as structured by professional boundaries as was my time with Jesse. He was always able to walk without using my body as a guide. In fact, he was more than careful not to overstep this boundary. He did not want his abilities to be in doubt, nor would he abide even the slightest innuendo.

During our brief walk down and then up the San Francisco hills, there is a strained casualness between us. I am aware of Isabel's hand on my arm and am sure that she is as well. As a psychologist, I have devoted a lot of time to considering the many meanings of touch and the use of space in different interpersonal and cultural circumstances. So much has been written about power and intimacy, gender and ethnicity, and the ways that they express themselves through touch. To members of cultures that touch more and come closer physically, Americans often appear somewhat cold and distant. To those who touch less than we do and maintain greater distance, we may appear too eager to be friendly. These national differences are always modified by personal power and by gender. In general, the more powerful individual initiates touch more easily. If a woman does so, her act is more likely to be interpreted sexually, as is a woman's body in general. In cultures that ban access to women's sexuality, there may be no touch permitted, in itself affirming the sexuality attributed to anything about a woman's body or appearance. In a world without sight, touch becomes more important and less taboo. It takes on a different meaning, matters in a different way.

Although Isabel has a blind dispensation from this complex cultural code, I, of course, do not and am experiencing both a slight loss of control and a too instant physical intimacy. I am planted firmly on my own mattering map (Kaschak 2010, 2011), on which touch is not instant or easy. For me, this is both cultural and personal.

"Where would you like to go?" Isabel asks. My usual preference would be to wander around a bit, see what kind of eateries are there and then choose the most appealing one. I have no idea if this is possible with Isabel and don't want to ask. I want her to be comfortable and as spontaneous as possible. The truth be told, I also want to escape the discomfort of touch and would prefer to find a place to sit and talk with a table between us. I am more like Jesse in this regard. I ask Isabel to choose a place and she easily finds the way to her favorite café, where we will spend the next couple of hours. I don't yet ask her how she was able to find the café without going directly to it on her usual route. Later, when I do, she will refer to it as "a neat trick." Isabel is full of "neat tricks" that create the illusion of sight while substituting for it.

I listen now to the tape of our first conversation that I made that day in the café. Isabel is asking me about myself and about my work. She wants to know about me before she tells me about herself. She wants a relationship to develop and not just to participate in a more traditional objectifying interview. I too want a deepening discussion and not a question-and-answer session. In this way what she tells me will not be stripped of context and more subtle meaning and nuance will be possible. I hope to bring the fullness of who we both are to our discussions. I say none of this to Isabel yet, although I will later on. For now, I answer her questions. I want her to be able to get her bearings, to decide how openly to talk with me, to place me on her mattering map (Kaschak 2010, 2011). She asks me a lot of questions, and, as I listen back in time, I think she is also drawing me out, trying to make me comfortable at least as much as herself. Her words and responses are quick and frequent, giving a staccato punctuation to my answers. She is working as hard as I am to create a connection, expressing interest in me and in my work. Later on I will realize that she also is making a statement about our developing relationship. It will be one of equals; she is not to be patronized or cared for except as and when she requests help. I silently agree to these terms.

Isabel asks where I am from originally, detecting a certain rhythm and pronunciation in my speech that is different from her own.

"Are you from New York?" she guesses eagerly. I am, and she is pleased to have been so accurate. This is a common way of trying to know someone by whatever initial cues stand out. I spent my earliest years in Brooklyn and then was swept up unwillingly in the mid-century migration to the suburbs in which my parents participated happily, their American dream coming true. Mine stayed focused on the cacophony, diversity, and density of city life, to which I returned as soon as possible. I never went back to Brooklyn, but I found what I was seeking and more in San Francisco and, later on, in Oakland, perhaps the Brooklyn of San Francisco. All these years later I still sound like a New Yorker to many people in California.

Learning what it means on each mattering map (Kaschak 2010, 2011) is what takes patience and a slower unfolding. I hope Isabel and I get there, but, for the moment, I appreciate her attempts to begin to know me through whatever information I make available to her. She asks questions that are a bit more concrete than is customary, a bit too direct, much like her eagerness for physical contact. She is a conversational reductionist. Such directness might be considered tactless in a sighted interaction and certainly more so in California than in my native New York, but how else is Isabel to gather the information she wants and to participate in forming the relationship we both want?

Soon we are discussing Isabel's early years, which could not have been more different from mine. True, she grew up speaking English, but a slower, more precise version than my speech. She is not in a rush to get her words out. I almost always am, as if everyone around me were racing by and could catch my words for just a moment before they move on. And that is the precise context in which I learned to speak.

Isabel was not born to be an outsider. Unlike me, she was raised in a mainstream Protestant family in the Midwest and homeschooled by her mother. But those blue eyes did not see. Without sight, she was instantly an outsider in this visually based culture. Also she realized in early adolescence that she was attracted to girls and not to boys, thus doubling her outsider status, struggling to keep her balance and to make a life on this precipice. She grew up in a family that would not accept her blindness, so what could they possibly have thought about her lesbianness?

I soon remind Isabel and myself that I began this study to understand, from the unique perspective of nonsighted persons, the role of visually based concepts, including race and gender, in sighted life. I am trying to explore language and the deepest recesses of thought and experience. I am asking about contrasting mattering maps, but use those words only to myself. I wait to see where Isabel will go with these ideas. I expect her to have a lot to say about gender, and perhaps sexual orientation, but she begins unhesitatingly with issues of color and race. I thought at first that she might be negating her own life experience, but this was not at all the case. I would later come to understand the central importance to Isabel of color, wherever it might be perceived, including on human skin.

In this way our conversation turns to a discussion of race and the dilemmas of black people rather than those of the blind. Isabel is going to try to convince me that she can perceive color even without vision or, at least, that she can understand just what it is well enough to grasp its meanings without the concomitant experience. I am listening carefully, as I myself don't know if this is possible.

As we begin to discuss race and skin color, Isabel separates them in a way that makes sense to her and, interestingly enough, to me as well. "Race is not really about color," she tells me. How would she know that? At the same time, I take her point. That is, it is and it isn't simultaneously. It could just as well be about some other quality that the eye perceives and that the mind can use to divide and to categorize, but it is not. Life histories have been defined and constructed on the foundation of skin color, supported and reinforced until it is not a shaky foundation at all. Lives have been destroyed over beliefs and prejudices that rest on the visual perception of skin pigmentation. Isabel and I are able to agree that cultures "racialize" and categorize individuals. In fact, along with other contemporary critics of the American racial system, I prefer the term *racialization* to race, indicating that we are speaking a cultural language and not a genetic one at all. It is human sight that creates this imputed "reality" and not the reverse, for what begins as perceptual discrimination ends as a more pervasive and dangerous form of societal discrimination. And it begins in the eyes of the beholder.

For different reasons from those of Isabel, I was something of a child philosopher. There were other circumstances of adversity in my own particular childhood that I tried to understand, along with the ordinary circumstances of human birth and death that confront us all. Many of us forget how much a part of childhood these questions can be, preferring a sort of retrospective romanticizing of those early years of life. In my own quest for understanding, I pondered everything from the existential to the empirical. I worried as much about whether to wear my saddle shoes to school as I did about the meaning of life or how I could believe that Russia existed if I had never seen it for myself. All these years later, I am still concerned with updated versions of these precise questions. Of course, my shoes are in keeping with current fashion and I have been to Russia, but, as for the meaning of life and the role of seeing for oneself, I still do not have the answers; the questions have deepened with years of living them. They have become old friends and companions.

Although I had not yet found the path that I would take through and out of the wild terrain named childhood, I was carefully creating it a step at a time. In retrospect I can see clearly where it was leading. This is the imputed inevitability of hindsight, when the story has cohered, the path forged and clearly marked. There were many turning points along the way.

Some I chose, and others chose me. Over time, a path has been worn, and it appears that I followed it rather than created it. In some combination of both, I suppose, I got here.

Isabel was compelled by circumstance to think about color in ways that I was not. As a blind person, she would follow the paths of mattering in her own direction and put the amalgam of experience and thought to her own uses. She would wonder, for example, how central the color of skin is to the idea of race and she would arrive at her conclusion on a less visual path than my own. I did not grow up pondering the deeper meanings of color, of the encoding of human skin, and thus I came to the discussion later than a blind person or a person of color might. But it is inescapably clear to us both that race has developed into an elaborate cultural code to a much greater extent than it is a material reality.

Isabel and I are interrupted by the arrival of our food and drink, a ham and cheese sandwich and coffee for her. For me, a Greek salad and my customary double espresso. As we continue to talk about color and race, I keep an eye on Isabel to see how she approaches the task of eating a sandwich in public. I can see that she relies on touch, although she feels that she has a "sixth sense" to guide her, and that this is a neat trick.

How did she first learn about race as a child? About skin color? Isabel tells me that she grew up in a racist family. For her father in particular, blacks, along with Jews, Catholics, and Democrats, were all a problem. We both laugh a bit nervously, but at what? The assumption that we disagree with him, see the error of his ways, have both chosen to live according to values that oppose these? The discomfort at even saying these things out loud? The unspoken and as yet unspeakable questions about me? I do fit somewhere on his list of abominations, maybe in too many places and too many ways. She has, for the moment, diffused the issue of color per se.

As a child, I learned that there was black skin and white skin, although my eyes saw shades of brown and a kind of pinkish yellow. In my set of crayons, there was a color called "flesh." It was a sort of pinkish orange, not really the color of my skin or anyone else's that I had ever seen. I associated it with drawings of people, but not with real people. I suppose I unconsciously assumed that it was only a symbolic representation of skin. I was on the right track.

In recent years, I have reflected at length on what a white person is. I have asked my students to choose sides in the color divide and I have done so myself. It is not so easy, not so black and white. They mix, in many combinations, into shades of brown rather than the shades of gray that optics dictate would come of black and white.

Here is some of what has emerged from these discussions. What is whiteness and what does it mean? Most students who identify themselves as white have never thought about this question. In the United States, it is the mainstream, the generic, the default position. It is ordinary and requires no special attention or explanation, no unspoken "Where are you from?" or "How did you get here?" Or "How did you get to be white?" It just is.

There are many international students in my graduate seminars. The North American eye easily categorizes them as ethnic minority people, brown if not clearly black. Yet most of these students, from countries as geographically diverse as Iran, Argentina, and Peru, are considered white in their own countries and therefore think of themselves as white. In some of their countries *white* is a code word (or an entry permit) for "upper class," and most of my foreign students do come from upper-middle-class backgrounds. Only when they cross the border into the United States do they instantly become people of color, the contemporary phrase for what used to be known as colored people. Only when they cross into the United States are they assumed by virtue of nationality not to be white. The American mattering map differs from those of their countries of origin and often confuses immigrant status with race. My students are shocked and disoriented to learn that they are no longer white. It seems entirely too arbitrary. They have been led to believe that race is something real in the sense that it is biologically based and invariant. It should not be subject to change as the result of a simple plane flight. After all, it is not about geography or crossing a border. Or is it?

Of course, people have different skin tones, but, as genetic research is beginning to demonstrate, this is largely a result of geography and not of genetics (Bolnick 2008; Cavalli-Sforza, Menozzi, and Piazza 1994; Sykes 2001; Jordge and Wooding 2004). Just as eye shape and nose formation are the result of adaptation over the centuries to differing climates, so is skin color. The additional meanings attributed to it are largely inventions of the human mind rather than naive discoveries of perception. Not just any mind, but the minds of people who have the power to make their perspectives and biases, their point of view, into the official map. The map creates the territory at least as much as the reverse. The country in which Isabel and

I grew up places what it names race in the center of the cultural mattering map. It does not rest there alone, but intersects frequently and predictably with gender, class, and even sexual orientation, as well as with too many other personal human qualities.

In my graduate seminar on ethnicity and gender, I sometimes ask two students to hold their arms side by side. When one is from a group named white, the other from a group named brown—let's say a Greek and a Costa Rican—it is not their skin color that distinguishes them, but the cultural ideas about Europeans and Latinos. The darker-skinned Greek person is a white person; the lighter-skinned Costa Rican a person of color. I myself am considered white in the United States, although my grandparents were not. They were Jews and therefore categorized as nonwhite, as were many other immigrant groups, including the Irish and the Italians. Only over the last three generations did we all become white, without our skin color ever changing.

By the time my ancestors were enslaved and then murdered, the government of Germany had not only weapons, but the emerging technologies of the assembly line, borrowed directly from Henry Ford, and an efficient process for tracking its citizens, contributed just as willingly by IBM (Black 2001). In the late twentieth and early twenty-first centuries, the methodologies of enslavement are only slightly less apparent, but also have their basis in the latest technology. They are also more visual. They can often go unnoticed, masquerading as "freedom of choice," expressed as preferences for style, for particular possessions as a personal statement, and for product preference. A certain kind of person uses a particular kind of computer, drives a certain car, and even eats certain foods. The media are as much an instrument of this propaganda as of entertainment. No thoughtful observer could deny that teen magazines and the Internet have become the purveyors of gender culture for those still learning how to see girls and boys, men and women.

It is a modern Western idea that each of us can exercise "choice." Don't I choose what shoes to wear, what brand of TV to buy, what group to dominate or enslave? Choice itself is informed by so many conscious and unconscious influences, by the same training that forms vision, that it is open to debate as to whether there even is such a thing as choice. This is a modern or postmodern echo of the Enlightenment debate over free will. Today, however, we know a lot more about psychology and neurology, and some argue that one's brain determines one's choices. Others claim that learning, from individual to cultural, shapes each brain, each pair of eyes. I am in neither camp, but have a foot in both. I do not find them false, but only partial. The map is multilayered. If the wind is blowing, the sands may shift.

Isabel's knowledge of racial issues is not based on her senses. It is all hearsay, a theory that she elaborates on a daily basis. She has never seen different skin colors, never even heard about "flesh colored" crayons. She had to listen carefully at home to learn not just the colors, but the meanings of these colors. Those of us who learned vision have these meanings embedded in our sight and do not have to think about them in every circumstance. Our eyes and our neural networks cannot but recognize them. But Isabel depends on other people's eyes and other people's meanings. Although she rejects some of these ideas, she cannot escape them.

In her father's world, a lot of time was spent figuring out who was Jewish, she tells me, and I wonder if she is trying to figure out whether I am Jewish. She doesn't ask, and I don't offer the information. I want to encourage her to follow her own thoughts as unself-consciously as possible.

"But what I carry around most ingrained in me are black-white issues," she continues blindly, never having seen either color. The comment about her father was a bit of a diversion and yet not one at all. She wants to be sure that it has had its desired effect of bonding her with me and separating her from him. To let me know that racism doesn't require sight. Or, more precisely, it requires someone's sight and someone's willingness to build an edifice of meaning on a false foundation.

Isabel's sister is also blind as a result of the same genetic anomaly that affected Isabel. Their parents, however, refused to accept material reality. Instead they pushed their two daughters to think in terms of color and in terms of sight. Despite all evidence to the contrary, these parents believed that, if the girls tried hard enough, they could see. Isabel retains to this day the odd habit of "trying to see" and of wanting desperately to understand light and color. She plays guessing games with herself and then with me, trying to develop an alternate way to see. She doesn't succeed and continues to disappoint her parents and herself. When a guess brings her close to the right answer, she is delighted and triumphant, a smile brightening her face. In a way she is right. Vision is a complex achievement. But, sadly, she is wrong more often than right. Material reality wins this argument hands down. She is pretending to see, a careful student of what a sighted person takes for granted and learns without effort.

Isabel continues describing her parents. "They love going on museum and art tours. They don't enjoy events like concerts where there is nothing to look at. They are very visual." She insists that she appreciates this quality in them.

"Colors are very important to my mother," Isabel says. "I know because she talks about them so much. She's told me that red is a good color for me, but I'm not exactly sure what she means. For example, I don't understand at all what different shades of color are, what the difference is, let's say, between maroon and pink." Isabel has spent a lot of time on this question, thinking about it and questioning friends who are art students. As a result, she has developed her "own theory," as she puts it.

"I pay a lot of attention to it because color is important in the sighted world. I don't want to say the wrong thing to anyone."

Isabel and her sister tried so hard to see, to please their mother.

"We wanted it so badly. Mom would describe something and tell us exactly where to look, and we would try. Sometimes I can see a flash of light. Seeing a tiny bit of light, a tiny fraction of some world that isn't mine is a neat trick and fun." She sounds happy describing it.

"It isn't really important to me," she adds with enough hesitation in her voice to indicate just how important it is.

I am struck by the callousness of her mother in forcing this untenable position on her daughters. If I were Isabel, I imagine that I would be both enraged and disappointed, but I cannot trust my imaginings of her life, so different is it from my own. Perhaps had I been born blind, I too would have tried to be a good daughter to compensate my mother and appease the gods.

Isabel only smiles as she continues with this line of thought. Clothing is also important to her. She is her mother's daughter. She wants a "different look" in different situations, just as I do. She has, by different means, learned the same code that I have. For her, it is more conscious, more of a challenge or a sport. "Being able to accomplish that takes a lot of sight to pull it off. Learning it has been fun. I have scored enough times to have some confidence." She launches into a series of stories about her shopping forays. For her, buying a flowered jacket and then a blouse and skirt that match it is a true adventure, and a source of immense pride if she "gets it right." I wonder who is in charge of making that judgment. Who is in charge of it for me?

"What would you want to see if you could see for twenty-four hours?" I ask a psychologist's question. Isabel has thought about it already.

"It would be fun to see how right or wrong my ideas are. To look at people, especially at women I've been in love with. But it would be very disconcerting also. Seeing the color red or seeing my cats would be a neat trick. But with people I would wonder if I could trust how I have known them as a blind person. Would I learn something about how sighted people see each other that I don't want to know? Or how I look that would be upsetting?"

And indeed it has been a shock to most blind people whose sight was partially restored through surgery. Oliver Sacks (1993) tells the story of a blind masseur who was so disgusted by the sight of human skin that he could not continue working with his eyes open. It was not at all what he had imagined. How could it be?

Isabel wants to talk to me next about her developing sexuality. She painfully remembers having had crushes on female teachers in elementary school. She recalls the feelings of intense longing that she had no idea how to acknowledge. "I can't have this," she thought. She already knew what she wanted and that she could not have it. Isabel was practically born knowing this. She is one of a large group of women and men who were aware of a strong same-sex attraction early enough in childhood to suggest to researchers a genetic basis for this orientation (Bancroft 1994; Mustanski et al. 2005), stronger in males.

Isabel seems to interpret my interest in gender to mean sexual orientation. No matter. These two qualities are frequently conflated by those who do not study the topic in depth. What she is saying is of great interest to me. I listen attentively to the story of her developing sexuality. I want to know how she experienced those years and how she has come to understand what she went through as she has, over the intervening years, elaborated and organized her experience to contain the meanings that are most important to her, her own mattering map.

She describes her childhood crushes in detail, the fantasies and the sense of longing and of the impossibility of fulfillment. What is so interesting to me is not that her crushes were exclusively on women, but that she responded to cues that were not visual. In fact, Isabel insists that even sighted people do not fall in love based on sight. This is only a partial truth, much like her insistence on the distinction between race and color. It is her own truth. I myself am not the only sighted person who has fallen instantly and irrevocably in love at first sight—and across a crowded room at that. I know it can happen, and not just in the movies.

Isabel continues. She is afraid that she will never find a partner because she is blind. She calls the problem "blind phobia," creating with her words a parallel to homophobia, although, as a psychologist, I would call neither a phobia. I would call them prejudices or fears.

She talks to me at length about the problem of dating. "Dating is so visual, the flirting and the eye contact. I just can't do it." It is difficult to imagine a successful first date without the glances or the prolonged eye contact, without exchanging smiles and with no subtle movement or visual cues of any kind. An entire language both subtler and more forthright than words is absent. The developing relationship must depend on the word, must be announced. This greater vulnerability necessarily bypasses flirtation, a mutual conversation, and perhaps more subtle invitation. I know that I could not do it easily, but I have a choice.

"Do you think only of dating a sighted person?" I ask.

"Yes," she replies without a moment's hesitation. "I would definitely want a partner who is sighted. Everyone knows that's better."

"Why is that?" I ask. I'm a little surprised to hear this from Isabel, given her sophisticated political analysis in other areas related to oppression and minority status. She's quick to answer.

"In the first place, they can drive and take care of other things that require sight. It is much harder to be alone in the sighted world." That makes sense. "And secondly, it has much more status to be able to attract a sighted person," she admits a bit sheepishly.

So Isabel doesn't discriminate against black people, but readily does so when it comes to the blind, including herself. Maybe in a truly blind society it would be the sighted people who would be considered of less status. That fantasy has been written about, most prominently by H. G. Wells (2011) in his short story "The Country of the Blind." I eventually find that almost all the blind people I meet are familiar with this story. It has to be irresistible for a blind person to imagine what the world would be like if everyone were blind.

Isabel has had a few short-term relationships with sighted women. Each time the woman left her because she is blind—or so Isabel believes. I understand that it can be a burden for a sighted person to have to negotiate so many aspects of ordinary life with a blind person. But I can as easily believe that Isabel seizes on this as the best explanation for relationships ending— and, for all I know, she's right.

However, I have underestimated the complexity of her perspective, because Isabel goes right on to say that a great fear of hers is that she is just not attractive enough. This is on her mind whenever she dates, as it probably is for most women. She tells me that she "tries to do it." She apparently considers attractiveness to be a variety of actions and not just physical characteristics. For her, race is not about color, and attractiveness is more an act than a quality. She is again both right and wrong. There are certain physical characteristics that are considered attractive in each culture. For women in the modern Western world, for example, facial features that are smaller and more like those of a baby are consistently evaluated as more attractive in many research studies. In general, a woman should be smaller in relation to any man with whom she appears. Facial features should include large wide eyes, a small nose, and symmetrical features. These are the characteristics that models and celebrities strive to achieve through dieting, makeup, and finally the technology of Photoshop. These techniques create the optical illusion of youthful feminine perfection.

Plastic surgery for women has for many years focused on eliminating ethnic variation from these standards, including altering Asian eyes to open wider and Semitic noses to appear smaller. Of course, these characteristics are combined with the confident and flirtatious performance of attractiveness, and that is what Isabel correctly feels she cannot execute, even with coaching. Not only can she not flirt or make eye contact, she cannot make up her eyes to appear larger or alter her body to appear smaller. Fortunately, her nose is an acceptable size and shape. Her blind eyes are blue.

I think about how important eye contact is to me and to most sighted people, especially in romance. It is essential in gauging the nuances of a developing relationship of any sort. It is how I know if I am making contact or not, being understood or not, appreciated or not. I cannot imagine any sort of relationship without it. Yet I will have to do just that as my friendship with Isabel develops. If the eyes are the windows to the soul, is there a doorway through which I can enter with Isabel, and she with me?

I don't comment about eye contact at this point, but instead talk about attractiveness. I'm so used to discussing this issue with women. Yet Isabel, I realize, lacks any context for comparing her "looks" to those of other women. The very word betrays her. She explains that she has found a way to do so, and I am surprised but more saddened at the realization that even she has not escaped this cultural mandate. Is this the eternal concern of women, even blind ones? Apparently so, as Isabel goes on to explain that she "can do it" by what she calls "a deep paying attention." She listens carefully to what is said about each woman and who says it. She pays more careful attention to those of her friends she knows are considered hip and attractive, trying all the time to figure out what it means to be attractive and how it works. She is a careful student of physical attractiveness, something she can never experience directly. She can never confirm her hypotheses, but only endlessly test them. Yet, even as a blind person, she cannot imagine attractiveness any other way. Isabel circles back to it in the most physical, visual sense. "It boils down to how the person looks." This leads her over and over down the same blind alley.

When I ask her about the women she has found attractive, she doesn't consider other aspects of attractiveness, as I hoped she would. Instead she replies proudly, "I am very good at figuring out what people look like from their voice and body size." Of course, I cannot resist the obvious question, "Do you have an idea yet of what I look like?" I consider that her wanting to hold my arm while we walked to the café had more than the obvious purpose, and this turns out to be true, as she has developed her hypothesis about my appearance from my voice, my comments, and the feel of my body as we walk together. She is both right and wrong, of course, but that is not as interesting or surprising as this early impulse to figure out what I look like without being able to see me. Isabel's brain offers her no visual imagery. Yet she acts as a member of her culture, wanting an instant evaluation of appearance and attractiveness. Everything in her but her eyes wants to fit in.

Her ideas about my appearance are not unlike her other hypotheses and theories: a bit too monolithic and concrete, but very perceptive. Yet they differ from Jesse's idea that I must look intelligent. She does not mention intelligence at all, but, much as Jesse did, turns instead to her own ideas about what matters in a woman's appearance. She can achieve that much even without sight. She knows my size and shape from walking close to me. My appearance, in her mind, is simple and straightforward, unadorned.

Isabel continues on the theme of gender. She knows a male-to-female transgender person. This friend's voice remained low even after surgery and hormone treatments. As a result, Isabel could not stop thinking of her as a man. Transgender surgery and hormone treatments change visible aspects of the body. To sighted people, the illusion is generally sufficient, although they may use other visual cues, such as hand, foot, and Adam's apple size, to make a gender assignment. Isabel hears only the unchanged voice, which can be altered somewhat by lessons in speaking "like a woman." A woman's voice must be higher in pitch, the tone more varied and lilting, sounding questioning rather than authoritative. In recent generations in the United States, a women's dialect has developed, sometimes called upspeak. Those who use it, mostly younger women, do not make flat-out assertions, do not sound too assured or confident. In spite of all the efforts of professional and business women to buck this trend, Isabel and others still assume an assertive "masculine" voice signals someone who is a man.

She tells me an interesting and related fact. Did I know that according to Randy Shilts (2011), the late gay male activist and author of the landmark book *And the Band Played On*, there is a disproportionate number of gay people in the military encryption corps? It makes sense that people who have had to learn a subtle and complex communication code would be good at encoding. And at breaking codes when life depends on it. So far, my opinion is that blind people would not do as well.

The hour is growing late, and I decide this is a good time to stop for the day. Isabel and I have had a lively discussion and we will have several more. I am already anticipating our next meeting as I walk her back home. She has given me so much to think about.

Going over the tapes at a later date, I notice something else. Isabel is trying to follow me, my questions and my timing, trying to laugh when she should, to discern my layered meanings without the cues of facial expressions. She is straining, trying. I also strain to lead the way and to be as precise and clear as I can. I attempt casual conversation, small talk, although it is not a size of talk that has ever fit me comfortably. So I talk a bit too much, and she laughs a bit too much. This has truly turned into another blind date.

4

Hiding in Plain Sight

Never bend your head. Always hold it high. Look the world straight in the eye.
—HELEN KELLER

ALL OF US LIVE ON multiple mattering maps along with physical ones. On mattering maps the terrain looks different in the eyes of each person because it matters differently to each of them. A mattering map is based on the complex cultural and personal values and experiences of each person. This concept, in different guises, is at the core of many psychological theories, including my own (Kaschak 1993, 2010, 2013.) Accordingly, coming to know another person evolves from coming to understand her or his perspectives and meanings—that is, what matters to the person. A relationship thus involves managing two different mattering maps, and this is what I am trying to do with Jesse and with Isabel. I am coming to see where our maps overlap and where they diverge.

In Costa Rica, where I have lived off and on for forty years, no one can read maps, although Costa Ricans are oriented in their own version of space and time. This makes it extremely difficult for first-world tourists, who have learned to depend on a two-dimensional, flattened, and decontextualized representation known as a map. When you show such a piece of paper to Costa Ricans, they shake their heads and don't understand, don't know which way to hold it. I have seen this more often than not. Turn the paper. Is Nicaragua up, down, or sideways? There are street signs in the capital to help orient you. They indicate left for Panama, right for

Nicaragua. There are no street addresses and thus no mail delivery in the usual sense.

Here is how directions might be given. "Continue on until you come to a sleeping dog. Turn left there and then right at the tree that was in front of the pharmacy that burnt down in 1948." You need history, geography, geology, good interpersonal skills, and a lot of patience to get anywhere. You need context and mattering (Kaschak 2010, 2012). You will ask again every few minutes, as the directions can change and so will you. Along the way, you will have made a lot of friends. You will be angry at some of them for giving you incorrect directions, but correct is not what matters most; a friendly response and participation in your journey is. And the mattering is inextricably intertwined with the matter or physical map. You cannot separate them even for a moment, and you will not get anywhere if you do not pay attention to both. What I am trying to do with Isabel, as we meet again, is to understand her mapping and her map.

A few weeks after my last meeting with Isabel, we make a date to meet again. This time I know the way and the color of the house. As I walk up the steps to Isabel's front door, I remember something that she has told me: all through her childhood, her mother encouraged her to try harder to see. I have never heard a more discouraging form of encouragement. Yet now I think of it in a different way. How hard it is for Isabel or any blind person to grasp that she cannot see, no matter how much will power or American "pull-yourself-upness" she exercises. Isabel will never be able to shout, "Mommy, I can see," even though her mother longs for it, prays for it, even demands it. Neither of them can make it so, this mother and daughter trying to perform miracles for each other and themselves. As I get to know Isabel, I can see the ways that she still tries and can feel my own wish for her to look at me just once. I am beginning to feel her longing as my own.

When we walk together, Isabel tries. She can see some contrasting light and dark, she has told me. "If I can see this much, why can't I will myself to see a little more?" she reasons. She has a sense of walls nearby, knows the place where space ends and solid begins. We are walking on a street that she has been on hundreds of times, so she knows these building walls not by sight, but by heart. Perhaps she is deceiving both herself and me in her adult effort to perform her mother's miracle. I do not yet know that it is the changed sounds echoing off the surfaces we pass that inform her. Like a seasoned magician, she will not reveal to me how she performs her tricks.

I know what to do when we arrive at the customary café again—where we will sit, how we will order, how to discuss the menu with Isabel. I know how to do exactly what we did the last time and am following her strategy now. I take comfort in the familiarity and predictability of the place on my own and Isabel's behalf. Yet my refuge in the familiar takes its toll on our conversation, which begins awkwardly, as we struggle to find our way out of the familiar and predictable landscape in which we are temporarily lost.

We both wait for me to begin the designated conversation, to ask a question about her blindness. It is my move, yet I do not move. I am trying not just to ask a series of questions. Isabel waits, her head perched precisely in the direction of my eyes, another neat trick.

Much as she did the first time, Isabel begins the conversation. She wants to talk about me. We discuss my life for a while, starting with a description of my new home in the East Bay hills. I love the green of the hills, the views from every window, the sight of sunsets over San Francisco Bay. Of course, I am instantly aware of just how visually based my choice of a home is. I talk about buying a couch (I told you I'm terrible at small talk), and she asks jokingly if I bought a picture to hang over it that matches. A visual joke of her mother's, I am sure. Nevertheless, I laugh reassuringly.

Finally we get back to our discussion of blindness.

"Let me tell you one of the things that I like about being blind," Isabel offers.

"The sense of discovery." She describes learning about a friend's apartment as I might describe traveling to a foreign land. She immediately translates for me just as I have done for myself, both of us too concerned that I understand through my own experience.

"It is like when you travel and can't read the street signs or recognize streets," she says, always vigilant to speak her second language and not lapse into her native tongue. Isabel is like an immigrant child in an American school. A note is carried home to her parents: "Please speak only English to this child." The child learns English and forgets the mother tongue. In Isabel's case, the mother tongue has never been her own. Her mother speaks a foreign language that she can only imitate.

Isabel continues to talk of adventure, of the anonymity of passing "invisibly" through city streets. She feels visible in San Francisco in a way that she does not in Berkeley, she tells me. What is she talking about? Is she ever invisible to others as they are to her? She assumes that people in Berkeley do not see or notice her, as they don't try to help her, thus ruining her adventure. She goes on to describe the unsolicited help, mostly from men, but immediately talks about how hurt they must feel when she rejects their help. She inevitably sees the other person's point of view first and foremost. A lifelong habit as a woman, a blind person, a blind woman. As the daughter of her mother.

As the psychologist I am, I try to help her reach for her own experience. Men take her arm in public, she tells me; they offer unsolicited guidance. Women do so less. We wonder together if women would do so more in "private" spaces. She insists that she is not frightened by this and does not feel hassled or endangered. No one has ever tried to hurt her. They are trying to be kind without really thinking about what kindness is. The intrusion makes her angry because she wants to be able to savor the pleasures of anonymity when she chooses and as she defines it. It may be akin to how I feel when I am in the middle of Odessa and an American in plaid Bermuda shorts approaches laden with maps, guidebooks, and cameras, shouting to his family in loud English. Or it might just be akin to how I also feel on the American streets as a woman.

I am beginning to notice that responding to Isabel, acknowledging her words, does not encourage her to speak further, as I expect it should from all my years among sighted people. Instead it stops her, so that our conversation is full of awkward pauses and false starts. This was also the case with Jesse. Mirroring and reflecting are more literally visual than I would have thought. These are interruptions and not elisions. Even with my therapist's skills, I can't provide easy transitions or a sense of focused interest only with my words. Facial expression, eye contact, and body language speak as loudly as words and tone. But in this room they are silent.

I ask Isabel about reading other people's emotions without being able to see their faces. I am thinking about this awkward aspect of our conversation, but I am also thinking of the cross-cultural literature developed by psychologist Paul Ekman (Ekman 1993; Ekman and Davidson 1994). His highly regarded work points to the consistency of the relationship between facial expressions and emotions in all cultures. The implication of this research is that we are neurologically wired to express emotions as we do, scowling when angry and smiling when pleased. No one must teach these expressions in any culture. They arise in infants in response to adult stimulation, often the mother's face. Yet, in recent years, this universality has been questioned (Barrett, Wilson-Mendenhall, and Barsalou 2014), and, after my own experiences, I must add my name to the list of questioners. Isabel has not developed these expressions and seems unable to learn them, hard as she tries. Jesse's facial expressions did not change very much either. Although he could see in early life, somehow he had forgotten this ability. More likely, the external cues were absent to him, as they are to Isabel. But what about the internal ones? Apparently facial expressions must be triggered by interpersonal cues and not by internal feelings alone.

Isabel mentions that she worries a lot about smiling appropriately, especially in photographs. Someone has told her of this odd modern American custom of smiling for the camera. I myself am often told by strange men on the street to smile because "things are not that bad." Sometimes they are right, sometimes wrong. So Isabel has learned to smile much the same way that I have. Yet she is certainly more eager to please than I am. And of course it is not the same at all; for her, smiling appropriately means passing, not pleasing. Passing each test as a sighted person would.

Finally Isabel mentions to me that she has just turned thirty. Her friends had a small celebration for her. I recall that thirty was my most traumatic birthday. I really felt that I was growing old, that life was mostly behind and not in front of me. Isabel's main concern is that she still does not have a stable relationship, a partner. She is wistful. As a woman and a lesbian, this is what she wants most. How many times have I heard this, even felt it myself? Blindness does not alter this wish, perhaps makes it even stronger. The poignance I feel extends to all of us who have longed not to be alone.

Soon it is time to return home. As Isabel and I walk down the busy San Francisco street, I automatically fall into one of my city customs—window-shopping. I chat about what is in the store windows, which stores have disappeared and been replaced over the years. I realize that Isabel cannot see them, has no idea what we are passing, and is instead intent on her own experience, her own adventure in navigation. She is walking through a completely different physical landscape than I am, although I am right by her side. There are no store windows in her landscape, no casual glances at passersby, no enjoyment of the profusion of flowers overflowing on the sidewalk in front of the flower shop. Her experience means sensing where there are walls, hearing the sounds of voices and traffic, passing as gracefully as possible through crosswalks, and, in general, grasping the geography of her own landscape. And she is proud of her ability to navigate this complex terrain. She has met a challenge successfully, while I have simply strolled down Fillmore Street.

Weeks pass, and then one day I find a message on my answering machine from Isabel. She tells me there is an exhibit of art made by blind people that I might be interested in seeing. I return her call enthusiastically and suggest that we go together. I casually offer to swing by and pick her up, combining it with errands that require me to have my car and to be in her neighborhood. She accepts, and we make a date for the next afternoon.

Riding across the bridge to meet Isabel, I repeat my nervous tendency to rehearse small talk so that I can do it adequately for the first few minutes. The traffic is light, the weather warm. What do these mean to Isabel? She experiences the feeling of warm weather, but not light traffic. Do these things matter in her world, or will she work hard to enter mine? And why am I rehearsing?

"What if I have nothing to say when I get there?" I worry.

When I get to Isabel's house, I test myself. I try to take my time, to make a few notes first, and only to go to the door when I'm ready. Someone in an adjoining house looks out an upstairs window, curious. I force myself to spend ten minutes in front of Isabel's house so that I arrive precisely on time and so that I experience fully what is going on inside of me. It is difficult. I am nervous, feeling the years of accumulated penetration by sight. I am being watched and will be interrupted.

"What are you doing out there? Come on in." I have been shaped by sight in ways that Isabel cannot begin to imagine.

At exactly the time we agreed upon, I ring the bell. Isabel takes a long time to answer and, when she does, comments on how punctual I am. She does not seem quite ready. I begin to walk up the second set of stairs inside the apartment and then stop in midstep. Does she know I am coming up? Does she want me to? I remember to ask, and she doesn't really answer, so I decide to wait at the top of the stairs.

I am happy to see her again. She would know this in an instant if she could see my face, but instead I have to tell her with words. They are awkward for us both and different from an exchanged glance that would say more.

Isabel leaves me standing there, does not invite me in or ask me to sit down. I can see into the house from where I'm standing. There is a bookcase at the top of the stairs; it is made of beautiful old oak perfectly preserved or restored. It is filled with books. I can see the living room and the dining room. Both have been carefully decorated with a trained eye and are aesthetically pleasing, open and filled with antique woods. She obviously lives with someone who uses her eyes carefully. I don't look any further, having already seen more of Isabel's home than she has. This doesn't feel quite right, although I'm not sure why. I feel more like a voyeur than a guest.

I am taken aback by this feeling. A voyeur, looking right through the opacity of blindness without permission. An uncontrollable perversion, this sight of mine, inadvertently cloaked in secrecy. But what can I do? Look away? Close my eyes? I feel an urge to confess, to explain, to tell Isabel everything that I am doing hidden away from her, hidden in plain sight. Yet there is nothing plain about it. I say nothing and wait. The next time we meet she will invite me to sit in her living room and to admire the view out the front window, which she has been told is stunning. San Francisco with its many hills and bayside location is filled with such expected and unexpected sights. Her house is on a hill, with a panoramic view of a bay that she cannot see.

Finally Isabel is ready, and I am roused from my moral dilemma and relieved of the irresistible temptation to see more than I should. This desire has caused me problems since early childhood, but as an adult and a psychologist, it more often has served me well. With Isabel, my invisibility to her contrasts with her hypervisibility to me. I can openly stare at her if I am so inclined. She will have no idea of what I am doing. It feels intrusive and unfair to me, and I am sure it would to her were she to know.

I want the experience of a car ride with Isabel, just as I did with Jesse. I want to learn more about her reactions and perceptions, her sense of orientation. I want to see how her internal map functions. We set out on the car ride to the art gallery where the Lighthouse for the Blind show is being held. San Francisco is a small and accessible city. The ride from any neighborhood to the downtown takes about ten minutes if there is not an accident, a fire, or a parade.

In the car, I immediately notice that something is wrong, something is missing, although Isabel seems perfectly comfortable and is chatting casually. As we drive down an always chaotic Mission Street, more like a third world Avenida Central than an urban American street, Isabel's conversation remains on an entirely even keel and unperturbed. Her speech patterns do not in any way reflect the pattern of traffic or my driving. There is no tension in her voice or her posture, no pauses in her speech as another car cuts us off or comes dangerously close. She has absolutely no reaction to my New York driving habits. She makes not a single comment about the sports car that I drive or how I drive it. She just comes along for the ride.

We are a long while getting to the Embarcadero, where the gallery is located. Market Street is closed for the construction of a new streetcar line. I explain why I am turning and where we are. I try Van Ness Avenue, turning right on California Street, a straight shot down to the Embarcadero. At the top of California Street, there is some sort of political demonstration. I cannot read the signs from where we are. The police are diverting traffic and another left turn places us right back in the third world again, this time in the midst of Chinatown. Like all Chinatowns, this one is noisy and hectic. To me it is extremely colorful—red, green, and yellow on all sides, flashing neon signs, and people rushing along in the narrow streets and alleyways. Isabel remains placid until we finally arrive at our destination.

As we navigate our way from the parking lot to the elevator and then to an escalator, stopping several times to check the building map, I am aware that I am talking much more than I usually do, that I am explaining to Isabel, at each step, what I see and what I am looking for. I feel an almost moral obligation not to delay, to divest my own landscape of every sight but those essential to our purpose. This way there is much less to have to explain and interpret. But it's not easy for me to ignore the environment. The lights, colors, shapes and designs, the shop windows and people rushing or strolling by all call out to my eyes to look. It is I who feel the tension of obligation. Isabel simply follows me.

I am trying to strip-mine the context of its complex codes and sights, faithfully joining her, as best as I can, in her encryption corps. I keep up a running commentary on where we are, why we are turning or taking an escalator, and what I see. It is completely impossible to describe even a fraction of what I see. I recognize this feeling of exhaustion from times when I have had to translate a conversation from one language to another as it is taking place. Little do I realize that my effort at simultaneous translation has only just begun.

After what feels like an eternity of escalators, moving sidewalks, and stairways, we arrive at the gallery, where I expect a respite from the explaining, the guiding, and the constant translation. I am more than ready to relax a bit, to have something particular to focus on in depth and maybe even in silence. Yet as we step into the gallery I cannot believe my eyes. The show, entitled "Insight," and mounted especially for blind people, proves to be sight-based in more than name alone. Although there are a few sculptures around, the walls are filled with paintings that no blind person can see.

The too eager gallery manager meets us at the door, proffering simultaneously a printed brochure and a sweaty handshake. I accept them both reluctantly. "Do you have one in Braille?" Isabel tries. "No. I'm afraid not. It was too expensive to produce," comes back the slightly less eager response. He apologetically produces an audiotape, but does not have a player. He somehow expects Isabel to have one with her, and, as it happens, she opens her bulging backpack and out tumbles a Walkman. He has only one tape, which means we must part ways—I to my visual world, Isabel to her auditory one. I leave the choice to her. I don't want to deprive her of her experience, but which one, her experience of the show or of being at it with me? After a moment of listening to the tape, she chooses me.

So my obligation continues. Suddenly my pack is heavier than hers, although invisible. I alter my focus once again from sense experience and contemplation to careful description. Here again is the odd burden that I keep feeling. Isabel will only know what I choose to tell her about the exhibit, so I can lighten up as I decide what to describe.

Isabel is remarkably quick at grasping what I am seeing, at translating into her own terms and back into mine. What a quick study this young woman is and how practiced in her own bilingual art. How eager she is to grasp what is just in front of her, yet entirely beyond her grasp.

As is her practice, she asks me a lot about colors, and I find myself trying to describe the yellowness of a lemon and the orange and purple of a sunset. I try with words such as bright, intense, hot, but, despite Isabel's nodding eagerness, I am sure that I fail at this impossible task. Why does she have to involve me in her struggle to see colors? I feel the weight on me of this guided tour. Soon enough I cannot go any further and resort to a strategy that several of my graduate students have mentioned at different times. Other blind people have told me about it too. They often know when sighted people do this.

One of my students resorted to this strategy when she took a blind man to Walmart. Reading every sign, describing every item, got to her and eventually she just pared down her description. Another student reached her limit going through every single coupon in a week's worth of newspapers.

She began skipping a lot of what she saw. It just takes too many words to describe even a moment of sight.

In each case a blind person is at the mercy of the stamina and goodwill of the sighted person, knowing that the guide is eventually not reading, not translating everything, but afraid that any complaint will reduce even further the generosity and energy of the sighted companion. And now here I am doing the same. Isabel must see through my eyes if she is to see at all. How generous can I be with the language it takes to break a code of a lifetime, to put it all into words. Yet it is precisely what I have been asking her to do for me. Don't I owe her the same effort?

I just cannot do it. It is overwhelming to my senses and to my mind, too much to ask of myself. Sight is a more elegant, immediate, and complex language, really impossible to translate literally. The effort to make it conscious is futile and almost unbearable. So I stop telling Isabel everything that I see. I cannot continue. Isabel must know, cannot miss the sudden skipping around, wandering to the sculptures where she can touch, where her senses serve her. Her senses serve me also and permit me to rest my eyes and my translator's mind. And I do.

We continue to discuss the art, neither of us acknowledging what has happened to us and between us. Soon we both have had enough. Right next door is a branch of Just Desserts, and we go there to discuss the experience over blueberry cheesecake. Isabel seems somber, even sad, as we speak of the surprisingly visual base of the show. Yet I can't be sure if I am right about her reactions. A lifetime of habit directs me to the look in her eyes, but there is none. As she pretends to look right at me, there is only opacity. No revealed emotion. No response to my eyes or my face. My earlier relief at not being scrutinized by blind eyes has slowly been replaced with longing for the subtlety of communication that sight permits. Words fail us both, even as we struggle to bridge the divide between us. There is really no way to do so. We are trapped in different universes, all the while seated at the same table.

On the drive back, Isabel does something that she didn't do at all on the drive downtown. She struggles to code where we are, what streets we are going down to return. I take Market Street; it is the most direct. On the way back to her neighborhood, she begins to give me instructions based on her ideas about where we are. I don't know if she is doing this because she has more confidence or less after our afternoon at the gallery. "Stop at the building with the flags," she tells me long before we are on the correct street. I have stopped for a traffic light, and she is guessing that it is the light in front of the large hospital, where I am to drop her for her next appointment. But we are still all the way over on Haight Street in an entirely different neighborhood.

Isabel must exhaust herself with a lifetime of paying attention so carefully. As I try to match her attention with mine, I am certainly exhausting myself. I am relieved when it is over, when I am again able just to drive, to walk, and to think silently. And I realize that this is precisely how I felt after the long drive with Jesse. Each time, I now realize, I have attempted the impossible. No wonder I am exhausted. Spending time with Isabel and with Jesse has made me see just how much I do see in an instant. The colors, shapes, textures, and sizes, the appearance of each person in my visual field, their clothing, demeanor, body language, the slightest flicker of a change in facial expression or eyes. It is impossible to have enough words and to use them precisely and rapidly enough to describe a single moment of vision. I, who have always treasured words, am coming to appreciate the complex language of sight. I have undertaken the impossible and have tried my best to succeed. I am stubborn that way. My success, although partial, lies in what I have learned.

In the beginning, Jesse and Isabel both easily tricked me. Neither one had malicious intent, not by any stretch of the imagination. On the contrary, they were both generous enough to invite me into their lives and to openly speak their second language with me. Both of them let me see their carefully developed tricks and helped me to understand their language, to which each of them has devoted a lifetime of learning.

Soon enough I began to get a glimpse of what I had come into their world to see. I was beginning to understand something new about the multiple meanings of gender and of race, but I was also seeing much more. At this point I had just a glimpse of what it was. I was beginning to see that sight was much more than just a language, although it is that; it is also a system of knowledge as complex as spoken language and developmentally preceding it. Where it comes to exist, it is the first language.

At the start I thought that the uses of sight were no more complex than those of the spoken word and that, if I paid attention carefully enough, I could translate everything I saw for Jesse and Isabel. More poignantly perhaps, I thought they would really be able to understand what I was saying, and, in my own naïveté, I undoubtedly contributed to their eagerness to pass.

I think I got the better part of the deal, but I hope not. I learned so much about the complexity and subtlety of sight. I was beginning to think about how sight became the basis of entire human systems of belief and knowledge that could better be called vision. Yet this is only the beginning. I will elaborate on these ideas as I come to know other blind people. Much more remains to be seen.

Looks Are Everything

SAMANTHA IS A SEXY BLIND WOMAN. She works at it. And I'm sure she would be happy to hear me say so. She had many affairs and sexual trysts before marrying, and she may be having them still when the opportunity presents itself. Which it does.

I first met her at a national conference as a colleague. She did an interesting presentation about couples' therapy, and, speaking with her afterward, I learned that she practiced in the area where I taught clinical psychology. We stayed in contact and, some time later, I invited her to supervise one of my graduate students. She accepted, and after several months I invited her to come speak to our seminar of therapists-in-training about her practice of sex therapy (yes, she has made a career of it). She would also talk about the early experiences that had led to her choosing this profession and why she was so good at it. Samantha had an excellent reputation for getting results in her work. Of course, the entire class was immediately fascinated and looked forward to meeting her. Hers promised to be a unique perspective, and everyone was eager to hear about it. We were not to be disappointed.

On the scheduled day and one full hour after the scheduled time, Samantha swept dramatically into the classroom alongside one bedraggled graduate student. Samantha had enlisted Lara's aid in helping her dress for the occasion, and this turned out to be a long, involved process. Thus the hour delay. Samantha was eager to make just the right impression and announced flirtatiously to no one in particular that it was her prerogative as a woman to be late.

Poor Lara, the graduate student in question, appeared completely unraveled and on the verge of tears, knowing that the entire class had been kept waiting. Samantha, on the other hand, was cool and in command. She immediately demanded and got the attention of the entire room, and she began speaking without waiting to be introduced by me or by Lara. We all struggled to regain our balance, although I'm not sure that anyone accomplished that for more than a moment during the course of Samantha's visit. I know I tried to regain control of my class with only moderate success.

Samantha has been blind since birth, as the result of having spent her first days in an incubator, a tragic circumstance that blinded so many premature babies until the cause of this misfortune—high oxygen levels—was discovered in the mid-1950's. Despite her lack of sight, Alexandra has managed to learn the special skill certain women have in making a grand entrance. Although she couldn't see them, all eyes immediately turned toward her in any room she entered. She not only knew this, she reveled in it. Hers is a kind of "in-your-face" refusal to be made to feel inferior to sighted women.

Samantha is forty-two years old; her skin is one of the colors that society names white, her sexual relationships of the nature that it names heterosexual. She is tall and slender with long light brown hair. On the day she came to class, she was dressed in a chic reproduction of a peasant blouse and skirt, one that no peasant could afford. In the course of the classroom conversation, she let us know that people consider her attractive and often make a special point of telling her that she is extremely good looking "for a blind person." You can see her pride when she says this. She revels in her own mastery of the sighted world and its definition of female attractiveness. She is exceptional.

Samantha has been married for several years to a sighted man, also an accomplishment in her world. She has snagged top honors in the mating game. She was about to demonstrate to our class almost everything about femininity and gender that we had discussed in earlier classes and that all the women in the room already knew in our bones. Her way of learning it was so much more conscious and deliberate than that of any of the sighted women in the room that it was a bit startling at first. By the end of the class, it is safe to say, the women in the room felt more similar to her than they did different. Although she has never seen herself or another woman, Samantha has mastered the art of femininity. Gender really matters to her. It is clear she is a sexy woman first, a sexy blind person second.

How does Samantha accomplish this feat? She leads with her sexuality and with a flirtatious charm. Unlike Isabel, she does not wait to be approached, but puts herself right out on display for everyone to see and admire. It is a kind of preemptive strike. Also unlike Isabel, who strives to become invisible, Samantha makes sure that she is the center of attention in any room that she enters, visible as possible. One strong influence, she reports, is that she grew up, like many other girls of her generation, reading *Seventeen* magazine, the Braille version of course. Just as Jesse had access to *Playboy* as a kind of training manual in becoming a man, Samantha studied the pages of *Seventeen* to learn to be a girl and then a woman.

As the pages of *Seventeen* told her, a woman adorned herself until her appearance was as stunning as the first flower of springtime. A man had only to look at her with appreciation and desire to decide whether or not to pluck this flower in full bloom. For them both, this was the basis of the gender contract. And it is one aspect of the sighted gender contract with which these blind men and women struggle to comply. They are both playing a game of blind man's bluff, a game that requires additional team members to help them play it well. Jesse has his visual memories; Samantha her teachers and friends. Both have the written media and auditory versions of the visual media to give them the necessary prescription. Samantha had an additional nudge.

She was raised in an Irish Catholic family with three brothers, three sisters, and two mightily overworked parents. These pious people readily accepted her blindness as "the will of God." They lived in an Irish Catholic working-class community in a small New England city where there was an entire culture built around the church. This included celebrating holidays and religious festivals together, sending the children to the church schools, and holding the priests and nuns, many of whom were from their own families, in high reverence as servants of God. In these schools little Catholic girls were taught to be pure and virtuous, to yield to the teachings of the clergy, and, most important, to safeguard their precious virginity for marriage and procreation. That is the formal teaching. There is an informal one that is much fiercer, which the world has been horrified to learn about, except for those fathers of the church who knew all along and kept this dirty secret to themselves.

Samantha's parents dutifully sent her to these religious schools, and the family attended mass every Sunday. In fact, it was their one outing together in a demanding work-filled week. There all the children of the local families were baptized and confirmed. In later years most of them either married each other or God at the very same altar. It was a holy sanctuary in otherwise busy, secular lives.

In that supposed sanctuary, Samantha underwent another ritual of baptism into holy femininity. She was sexually molested by her priest when she was seven years old. It continued after classes for several years, this violation of the holy sanctuary of her body and soul. Sadly, so many girls and boys undergo this cruel initiation ritual that it seems almost as ubiquitous as the official kind of baptism. How do they come to understand this violation by those whom they have been taught to trust as much as God himself? There are a variety of unsatisfactory ways to compromise with reality. Many use their bodies rather than their minds or hearts to make sense of this otherwise senseless experience. They hide their conclusions from no one but perhaps themselves. Some become asexual, but many more become hypersexual, and the females become what most of us would consider to be hyperfeminine. This version of femininity carries within itself the wound to itself.

These girls and women lead with their sexuality, almost as if the process of initiation confers on them a certain power over men rather than the opposite. Many can even describe this distorted sense of power. Such a sexualized approach is almost a sure sign of an early violation. It is a child's solution to an adult problem. Such women learn to equate their value and power in any relationship with their command of sexuality. They have learned their lessons well and keep repeating them as another child would the multiplication tables, believing that their sexuality gives them a magical "after the fact" power, as if they were actually in charge of their own molestation.

Samantha did not say any of this to us. She only enacted it. Yet, in my many years of practicing psychotherapy, I have had this discussion or seen it performed without words too many times not to recognize it. What Samantha did say, however, in the course of the classroom discussion, was that she connects danger with attractiveness. This requires no nuanced psychological interpretation. It is just too obvious and too bad. Early experiences of violation are always formative, and people make sense of them in a finite number of ways. Samantha's is not atypical. Among women who organize their lives around sexuality, many have been molested, raped, or otherwise sexually traumatized. Their behavior is a failed attempt at mastery through enactment and it serves to keep the injury alive as much as it keeps it out of awareness. Samantha's history led her to focus on mastering "sexiness" and not worrying so much about blindness. The blindness made it just that much more complicated, but was only a modifier in her quest to be "sexy."

Samantha herself said nothing more than that she found scents like men's colognes and shaving cream stimulating and somehow invoking danger. It does not take a psychologist to guess where she first smelled them. I wish it were a rare enough occurrence that it did require some digging and interpretation, but it is so common as to be almost obvious. Of course, I did not choose to pursue the subject in front of the class that day. I was not sure that Samantha would feel free to say "No" if I asked her permission first, not sure if she knew how to say "No" in such a circumstance. And I could not judge her feelings by noting a flicker in her eyes or a nuanced expression move across her face. Nor could she judge my intentions in that same way. I decided to leave it to Samantha what she did and did not reveal to us.

What she decided to discuss next easily captured everyone's interest for the rest of the class session. She offered us a detailed description of the fine-tuning of blind femininity. Samantha had decided to protect her parents from the knowledge of what had happened to her on the church altar. She could clearly see what she could not literally see, how overburdened they already were, and decided to bear her cross herself. Silent, but not passive, she began to plan her own destiny in this world with the tools that she had been given.

She asked her parents to send her to charm school for blind girls. I don't know how she found out about such schools, but they are apparently not uncommon. I have heard tales of this kind of finishing school from sighted women. They are the slow learners, requiring a special school and a major in feminine charm. At charm school Samantha would learn that there was a special way for a girl to walk and sit, to move and speak. This is exactly what she wanted to know. She practiced walking with a book on her head so she would stand up straight and not "bounce around." Samantha's mother had complained that she walked "like a football player," but of course Samantha had never seen a football game and had no idea what this meant. Why shouldn't she walk in a way that felt free and happy, swinging her arms and bouncing up and down? Her mother explained as best she could that girls were supposed to walk and move differently from boys. What felt natural and easy to her was the boys' way. To become a woman took more study and more work. It did not come naturally.

I remember that when I was about six years old my mother sent me to ballet classes to learn to be more graceful. As I was an excellent athlete, I wondered for many years what she meant. And I probably never did learn to master what she considered to be grace. I both could not and would not. My body would not perform a tour jeté, nor would my mind permit it. Nevertheless, I performed my own version of these tortuous movements on the stage in the annual ballet school recital. It gave me no sense of power or control. I must admit that I enjoyed the attention, but not what I had to do to get it. It was just not my way.

Samantha could not afford to be too much of a rebel and instead chose her own route. In her determination to be accepted in the sighted world, she practiced and learned the skills that sighted girls and women breathe in every minute of every day. She learned to stand up straight, to walk gracefully with smaller steps, more like a ballet dancer than a football player, and, most important of all, to sit with her legs together. This was a must. She was learning both to contain and display herself and to take up less space. She was becoming a woman.

"I didn't have anything to mirror, so I had to be told and then shown," she tells us with a certain degree of satisfaction in learning her lessons so well. She knows now how to hold herself in a closed up position, occupying as little space as possible and presumably taking responsibility for her own safety, as this posture is supposed to indicate that "she is not asking for it." Despite these efforts, she was acquaintance-raped once and able to "talk her way out" of three other attempted rapes. She describes some of these situations to us in detail. Most took place in her apartment when she was somehow alone with a man who was a friend or a casual date but who decided to end the evening by forcing himself on her. Each time she was able to fight back or talk her way out of the situation.

Is this number of close calls higher than that of the average heterosexual woman? Would a man inclined to sexual aggression consider a blind woman an easier target? Is Samantha confused about what visual messages to send? It's hard to know without being there in her bedroom. In any case, she is no way complicit in her own violation as a result of her blindness, as she is still able to say "No." She herself believes that her attractiveness is at the root of this endangerment. She is irresistible in some mysterious yet satisfying way.

Her opinion engenders a long discussion in the class about whether or not unattractive women get hassled or attacked by men. Opinions vary. I do not have to tell you Samantha's position. Yet, in reality, all kinds and degrees of attractiveness do not protect girls and women from violation. Eighty-year-old women in nursing homes are raped by staff members, as are six-month-old babies, sometimes by their own fathers. Bosnian women are raped by Serbian soldiers and then again by the United Nations "peace-keepers (Sharratt 2011)." I will not continue with these examples. They are all too numerous. By now we know all too well that this form of assault has nothing to do with attraction or attractiveness. It is a form of violence unique only for the particular assault weapon and, if it is provoked at all, it is simply by the act of walking around in a woman's body. For Samantha, that is a sort of cold comfort.

Samantha learned about makeup in charm school. Apparently, according to her, using makeup is growing more and more common among women in the blind community. By this time, I had become used to blind people, women and men, not wearing dark glasses or shielding the sighted world from their sometimes quite distorted eyes. In the beginning it was difficult for me to look at them, as I tend to be squeamish. But I must admit that defining and outlining blind female eyes was hard for me to fathom. Would it make her more attractive to a sighted man? Would it make her look more like a sighted woman? How could she learn to master this dubious art?

Samantha was happy to explain herself. She prepares to go out with the help of a sighted female friend. The preparation begins in her clothes closet, where they put together an outfit. It then moves on to the choice of hair-style, and finally makeup, which is applied by this friend. Shoes are very important. Back when she was in school, some of the other girls took on this responsibility. They told her that her mother was dressing her differently and that she should change from bobby sox and loafers to nylons and heels. Of course, she did. Samantha has always wanted nothing more than to fit in.

Lara tells the class that Samantha has asked her to serve in this role several times. She did so reluctantly. And why was she reluctant? Not because she considered any of this costuming odd. In fact, it made perfect sense to her, as she was also a woman who took great care with her appearance. She was reluctant because she took all this so seriously that she felt uneasy assuming responsibility for "the look" of another woman. She was afraid that she might fail Samantha and let her own "look" intrude. She did not question the necessity of "the look," nor did Samantha.

Lara also told the class about an incident that had caused her severe discomfort and embarrassment. We all had to laugh when she was finished, although she was dead serious. Once Lara came to Samantha's house after dark to pick her up for a shopping trip to the local mall. The door was unlocked, but no one answered, so, after several knocks, she opened the door, walked in, and began to look around for Samantha. After a few minutes of walking through the living room and hallway, she found Samantha in her closet with a blind friend, choosing an outfit to wear. They were doing this with the help of an elaborate system of Braille labels and tags. The tags, attached to each piece of clothing, described the item and indicated what other items it could be worn with. Lara had actually helped Samantha set up this system.

There the two blind women stood completely in the dark discussing the colors, trim, and design details of the clothes in the closet. Samantha obviously had forgotten to turn on the lights in the closet or anywhere else in her house, so engrossed was she in her task. And why should she remember? For the sake of the sighted people around her, of course. How else would any of them even know that she was at home? How could Lara find her? The only apparent handicap in that situation was Lara's need for illumination. Yet even Samantha's neighbors had complained about the house being dark all the time. They thought it might attract burglars. The house itself was "asking for it." Of course, the whole episode gives new meaning to "coming out of the closet."

Later, when I visited other blind people, I found paintings or photographs hanging on the walls of their rooms for similar reasons. At least, this is what they tell me. "These pictures are for the comfort of the sighted people who visit me." Some of them go on to insist that they themselves like and can appreciate the pictures. When another blind woman, Andrea, claimed that she knew what each one depicted, I asked her to give me "the tour." She turned out to be wrong about every picture, just as Isabel had been wrong about the color of her house. I didn't challenge Andrea any more than I had Isabel. I didn't want to destroy her dignity, but my question had been answered. However, I am not sure that she really appreciated my question and would not have preferred a simple compliment about how nicely she had decorated her home. She had put so much effort into passing that my questions may have struck her as embarrassing and impertinent. I was the one who did not fit in.

Andrea is a blind woman who was very cordial to me, but after a few visits she called to say that she did not want to continue meeting. I was disappointed, of course, but could not convince her otherwise. In fact, Andrea was Jesse's girlfriend. She told me this as soon as I met her, although he had only called her a friend (as I mentioned in chapter 2). She was the first blind person who invited me to her home, and I was fascinated. Her apartment was simply and comfortably furnished, as it turned out, by her mother. She lived alone and cooked, cleaned, and took care of herself, although she did not have a job. Twice a week she cooked dinner for Jesse, and he spent the night. Once in a while, he cooked, but he didn't like her to come over to his apartment, which he said was "too messy." He had never permitted me inside either for the same reason, which he always insisted was a function of his gender and not his blindness. Jesse liked to save face.

I visited Andrea two or three times at her home. She preferred to meet there and not outside. On one of those visits she took me into the kitchen to show me how she prepared a meal. All items in the refrigerator and pantry were labeled in Braille. When it came to measuring and combining ingredients, she would place the index finger of her left hand inside the bowl or measuring cup to indicate when she had poured in enough of the item. As I got to know more blind people, I was treated to this demonstration many times.

I must admit that I am a bit fanatic about germs and often check to see if people wash their hands if they are cooking for me. I didn't come by this quirk naturally, but as a result of a long illness that has affected my immune system. Yet I wear it now like a glove. Not all of my blind hosts washed their hands, but no one ever actually cooked for me, so we were both saved the embarrassment of my unvoiced request.

There was always a sort of tension between Andrea and me. I couldn't get us beyond it, although I tried. Soon enough, Jesse reported to me that they had broken up, and, at about the same time, Andrea also severed her relationship with me. Jesse and I continued to be friends. I can only imagine that I contributed to a problem between them or at least somehow got caught up in it. Andrea always thought of me as Jesse's friend and maybe she wanted a clean break. Maybe she was jealous of our friendship. Maybe she just met someone else. I never did find out.

Samantha, of course, lives with a sighted man and has sighted clients who come to her therapy office, so she too has artwork on the walls. She especially likes seascapes, forest scenes, and sunsets; she is sure that she can "feel their energy" and so does not have to see them. This is an explanation that can easily pass muster where she and I live, in Northern California. In fact, there do seem to be certain intuitive persons who can, without seeing them, feel the energies of objects. This is not as strange as it sounds, since what appears to the human eye to be an object is more accurately an amalgam of electromagnetic waves. It is, after all, only our human sensory systems that organize our world into discrete and identifiable objects. But this kind of acute perception is not a common skill or, at least, not commonly developed, even among the blind. When it does emerge, it is often the byproduct of years of spiritual or consciousness practice (Pearle 2013).

This extraordinary skill is rare enough to have been studied in controlled settings by psychologists and parapsychologists. I have tested my own hunch by asking most of the blind people I know to describe colors or "the feeling" of a painting. As I had anticipated, not one of them could do so with any more accuracy than I can with my eyes closed. Many of them are annoyed by this stereotype of blind sensitivity. However, most blind people do try to develop their other senses as much as possible. Anyone would in this circumstance. But as far as being conferred extraordinary perceptual abilities, I think not.

I have glossed over a lot of Samantha's sexual adventures, which I want to describe in a little more detail. Not surprisingly, she has had several affairs outside her marriage. She is happy to talk about them, but does not mention whether she and her husband have an openly acknowledged agreement about this issue or not. And no one asks. From what I know of her though, I would guess not, if for no other reason than that such openness would surely remove the stimulation of the danger involved.

Samantha recounts the details of one of these affairs, albeit a failed one. She was at a conference for blind people and met a man who interested her.

It was apparently mutual. In the course of being together during the day, they decided upon an early evening rendezvous in Samantha's room. They agreed to meet at the hotel elevator at seven that evening, when the formally scheduled events of the day were over. Samantha waited and waited for him by the elevators, but he did not arrive—or so it seemed. She felt disappointed, hurt, and humiliated. When she questioned him the next day, he had the same reactions. It seemed that he had been there and that she was the one who had stood him up.

There turned out to be an explanation that solved this mystery. After agitated discussion, they both realized that there were two banks of elevators in the hotel lobby. While he was standing at one waiting for her, she was in front of the other waiting for him. Although they stood for an entire half hour only a few feet apart, neither one had any way of knowing that the other was right there. No other sense helped them find each other. So much for the scientifically touted role of scent and pheromones in attraction. Of course, this one unplanned incident proves little or nothing theoretically. Its poignancy may be its primary feature.

One more issue Samantha discussed with us that day in class struck me as humorous and, at the same time, also poignant. It's not something I would have thought of until she brought it up: the difficulty for a blind woman of having a menstrual period. She relies on her sighted husband to check her clothing before she leaves the house. During the rest of the day, she must rely on herself, and not always successfully. When Jesse had a large spot on the front of his shirt one day, I certainly thought about the issue of cleanliness as the sighted world defines it. It is impossible for blind people to know if their clothing is spotted, if the ketchup from lunch is on their shirt or on their face, if something is in their hair or nose. Never mind the more subtle spinach between their teeth after eating a salad. But blood on the back of a skirt seems to me to be the ultimate challenge. I suppose that blind women could choose to wear red or all black on "those days." I suppose that their way of checking without the help of a sighted friend or partner would be similar to their cooking methods. Yet why care at all but for the sight of the sighted?

I have had the opportunity to meet with Samantha another time away from the class. There is a new library in San Francisco serving the disabled community, and she wants to check it out, in particular their collection of audiotapes. I tell Lara that I will take her there. I want the opportunity to spend some time alone with her. When she tells me that she will meet me there, I do not insist upon picking her up. Samantha has her own ways of traveling. We meet in the lobby at an appointed time, and she arrived with her recently acquired guide dog. Maxi. Not only does Maxi make life easier for Samantha, but he draws more attention and comments her way. Samantha revels in this attention. The three of us head for the elevator that will take us to the room we want to find. The rooms are labeled in Braille for her and with clearly written signs for me. Both of our immediate needs are met.

The library itself will not be as easy to navigate, as they attempt to serve all the officially designated disabilities in the same set of rooms. Samantha is in search of books-on-tape. This is several years before iPods and other such devices; all these readings can now easily be downloaded on a home computer. This was still the Dark Ages of the 1990s.

We approach the librarian for help. It turns out that this young man is deaf. He can sign, but I do not understand this language. Certainly Samantha cannot. The deaf and the blind inhabit separate universes.

To accommodate us, he picks up a pen and paper and begins to write down his instructions and comments. The only communication possible between Samantha and him must go through me; I must use my visual and auditory senses to pass information back and forth. He writes his comments to me and I speak them to Samantha. Then she gives me her responses or asks other questions, which I write down and pass along to him. It is my own hearing and sight that permit me to serve as intermediary, the medium for their messages. I am once again a translator, trying to perch on two different sensory maps at the same time. Normally these maps work in tandem, in complete harmony for me. Tearing them one from another leaves me as shaken as if the rending were literal, as if someone had reached into my brain and disentangled the neuronal pathways. To separate what I have always known together is much more difficult than I could have imagined.

Samantha also feels the tension of the situation and clearly resents the need for my help. As we leave, she begins talking about this tension somewhat obliquely, referring to people who do not speak English and the impediment and difficulties that causes her. They are a problem, and she is just a regular American. It is clearly from her personal sense of bewilderment that she speaks this way. Had she been sighted, she would have been one to learn a bit of these languages and to champion their very diversity. Without sight, she already has enough translation to do in the course of an ordinary day. And Samantha does not like to be reminded of what she cannot do.

She and I talk a little more this same afternoon about gender expectations. Samantha has thought about this issue a lot and is very interested in feminism. She believes, as most of us who have thought about it do, that gender expectations are taught every day by the media.

"It takes blind people longer to learn them, but we do." Although interested in the gender expectations that feminism has brought to the fore in recent decades, Samantha is equally proud to be able to grasp and conform to these expectations. It is her own brand of feminism, I suppose, and the alternative to being an outsider. In her mind she does not miss the mark. Without even seeing where she is going, she is able to get there.

Of course, Samantha is not aware of the hundreds of visually based calibrations that each sighted person makes in response to eye contact, facial expressions, or body language. She cannot know how much even a single glance or gesture may convey in its detail or timing. The effects on another person of a slightly raised eyebrow or a completely raised one are almost too complex to put into words. And yet this is precisely what I have tried to do with each of these blind people. The truth is that only by trying and failing over and over did I come to this knowledge. Isabel has no more idea of the colors of a sunset than before I tried to describe one to her, and Samantha is just as unknowing about the myriad subtle and not so subtle glances of lovers.

Samantha's repertoire of gestures is limited to what she can commit to memory; she is not a native speaker of sighted language, nor is she fluent in it, no matter her seeming mastery of at least one important aspect. Instead she, like the other blind people I already know, is a lifelong student of the sighted relationship.

If that is so, then I myself am a captive of that same practice. As much as I try to develop these relationships and to be sensitive to the different perspective, I cannot find a way to breach the gap between us.

"What do I mean by this?" I ask myself.

The mirror does not reflect. As much as I try not to, I am looking for feedback in the eyes and on the faces of blind people. Do they like me? Are we connecting? Am I understanding? Are they understanding me? And I cannot find the answers anywhere I look. Where am I when I am with Samantha or Jesse, Andrea or Isabel? I am unmoored in some very disturbing fashion. I am disoriented in a way that none of them seems to be.

I am coming to realize that vision is crucial to my own understanding of each of them, and myself in relationship to them, but it is absent and unavailable. I find that I feel lonely. As much as I was initially relieved getting to know Jesse when I realized that I didn't have to meet the demands for eye contact of an ordinary sighted conversation conducted across a café table, I was beginning to miss the unspoken and nuanced intimacy of the very same act. And I was coming to understand how much I depend upon visual cues to know where I stand with another person.

Even more unexpectedly, I was feeling psychologically clumsy. I could not get my bearings. There were interruptions in our conversations or silences that were too long. There were my tension-reducing attempts at humor, which would be taken literally and thus wind up increasing tension. Nobody could see that I was smiling or perhaps had a slightly raised eyebrow. And I began to notice more and more, as I searched for the customary cues upon which I, a sighted person, depend, that the subtle details of facial expression and gesture were also missing. Although experts in nonverbal communication hold that facial expression of emotion is consistent and universal, I was not finding this to be the case. It is not that these blind people had a different set of facial expressions, but that they had none in circumstances where I expected them. Better said, their nonverbal expressions and gestures were reduced to the broad and the basic. They were not really serving as interpersonal calibrators except in the most general sense. These blind people undoubtedly were accustomed to this absence and perhaps could not even fathom what was not there and had never been there for them. I, on the other hand, felt a certain conversational vertigo; this was an entirely new experience for me. An entire language, crucial to me, was not being spoken. Without that language, where was I? And more important, who was I? Clearly not the same person I was in the sighted world. I was awkward in areas that I usually was not, confused about things I could generally see clearly, and a partial stranger to myself. This I had not expected.

It was I who was, more than they, in the dark, as the expression goes. Only those of us who know light, after all, can experience its absence. Although the sighted tend to imagine the nonsighted as being in the dark, that very image is based in knowing light. The blind reside in a zone where neither light nor dark exists. They can only sometimes extrapolate very broadly from their access to the other senses that remain intact. None of us who is sighted can imagine their world fully, and I was coming to understand that neither could they really understand ours.

For Samantha in particular, and blind people in general, vision must be imagined. For them, it is achingly central and does not exist at the very same time. As I try to master this incompatible duality, their map is little more for me than a huge blind spot. For Samantha and the others I have so far come to know, the map is one of extrapolated meanings and ideas, guesses and hypotheses. It is not informed by sight, but by a combination of other senses, hearsay, and what I had come to know as the process of passing. It was a different map in this combination than I had ever encountered before.

"Yet is this so different from my own sighted maps?" I still wondered.

The most important concepts that Samantha uses to organize her life seem to involve gender, femininity, and sexuality. These matter most to her (no great wonder). The precise framework she has created goes something like this. "Being a desirable woman is much more significant than being blind. I can be as desirable as any other woman and I can be in control of sexualized relationships. In this way, being blind comes to matter less." It is not a bad strategy, given the tools she possesses.

Within this dance of gender and sexuality, blindness and danger, Samantha finds the part of the blind man to be even more difficult than her own. She herself is better off, she rationalizes.

"Sight equals power for men," says Samantha, without explicitly saying, "Sex equals power for women." She has said it in every way except with words. She has a close friend named Luke, whom I will meet very soon. He is also blind and is a computer expert. He specializes in instructing other blind people in the technology—and there is an ever increasing amount of it—devised to extend their intact senses prosthetically. Samantha and Luke have an ongoing dialogue about blindness and how it affects masculinity and femininity. They both feel that being blind is, in general, harder for men than for women.

"Blind men are stripped of what it means to be a male, to be able to establish eye contact, to flirt, to pour a glass of wine." Samantha is truly Samantha, even in this circumstance thinking first and foremost about sexual encounter as the defining element of gender. Yet I too have come to realize how important flirtation is for most beginning sexual relationships and nearly impossible without the complex language of the eyes.

Of course it is possible just to say flat out, "I am attracted to you. What shall we do about it?" This does not compare with the subtlety of the dance of pursuit. It lacks the building tension that is so much a part of the early pleasure in this kind of relationship. Or, at least, anticipation of the moments of its release fuel the exchange. The glance. Looking away. More boldly making eye contact. Not looking away. All these moves becoming more and more highly charged as they continue and are reciprocated. Luke and Samantha can never know the pleasure of this sort of interplay, which engages the heart of desire. If they replace it, there is no way for them to tell me or seemingly for me to know from my vantage point outside the experience. I suppose that I could have begun a sexual relationship with a blind person, but that might have been going just a little too far for the sake of research.

However, I did ask Samantha one more bold question about sexuality since it intruded itself impertinently in my thoughts. I will eventually ask other blind people and get a variety of interesting answers. I want to know if sexual intercourse was surprising the first time, since she did not have the overwhelming visual bombardment of imagery that has grown so common in contemporary visual societies, where every manner of sexuality is visible on the Internet, in film, and even more uninvited in its unsolicited use to engage our attention sufficiently to sell a previously unrelated product— a car or coat or dishwashing detergent. Did Samantha know what to expect of sex, what went where and how, not having seen it first? I am asking now about the simple mechanics of the act, the "Insert part A into part B" of sexual intercourse.

I catch her a bit off guard. She does not seem to know about the sexual images all around us, selling not just sex itself, but material objects and ultimately a sense of self. Samantha pauses and thinks for a moment or two, then gamely begins to describe her first time to me. In fact, she says that it took several times until she got used to the details of anatomy for which she had not been prepared visually. She means that she did not really know about male erections or the precise mechanics of intercourse, the what-goes-where and how of it. She covered her inexperience by pretending to be prepared. Her strategy was and is to try to pass, "faking it" in a way completely different and entirely identical to that of many sighted women. It is a human strategy that perhaps comes in the package known as language. Perhaps the lie is born with the ability to speak, especially to oneself, and that is why the nonverbal is so important to the understanding of meaning and even truth. Words can deceive in a way that actions often cannot.

By the time I meet Samantha, I have already seen several different blind performances of passing in the sighted world. Samantha's unique contribution to my growing understanding was probably to demonstrate the precise details of flirting and of sexuality and how to approximate these skills for a sighted audience. Of course, her blind performance is a bit stilted, lacking the spontaneity and fine-tuning of visual exchange, the ongoing conversation known as body language and eye contact. She is less interpersonally reactive. Her communication is based, to a greater extent than for sighted women, on memorizing her lines like the lead character in a play. In each circumstance she gives the same command performance that she learned in rehearsal. It is stripped of calibration and context, but perhaps not of desire. And it is quite recognizable to the sighted.

Samantha had to commit to memory the details of gender as young children memorize the multiplication tables or as she herself has learned what clothing goes with what. The mirror does not reflect; no image stares back at her. Nevertheless, she is ensnared in the cat's cradle of vision. With the assistance of the written and visual media, the translation of sighted individuals, and the acts, both ordinary and obscene, of sighted men and women, Samantha has acquired access to the encrypted codes of gender. The performance remains a bit awkward but is recognizable to the sighted. Sighted performances appear smoother and better choreographed, but even they are filled in by the blind spot of every observing eye until they appear seamless and never upside down.

Samantha and Isabel, Andrea and Jesse must theorize and hypothesize gender and sexuality, sexual orientation, and an imitation of sighted flirtation. They are like scientists before Leonardo, depicting the insides of the human body without ever having seen them, and like explorers of the fifteenth century with their crude, yet imaginative, approximations of mapping. Their concepts are as much a part of imagination as of vision. Yet is this any different from the sighted depictions of these same concepts, or are the latter just easier to ferret out?

As I write these words on my computer, I look up to see the view from my office window. The sunset over the bay. A ribbon of red underlining the border between sky and land, a crimson horizon that gives me the sense I can see all the way out to sea—all the way to Japan even. An endless expanse. The tiniest sliver of a moon disappears behind a California cypress tree. As I write these sentences, I remember my childhood, the sense of possibility I felt then. If I dig deep enough, I'll hit China. If I stare long enough across the Atlantic Ocean, I'll see Europe. I imagined myself crossing those waters some day. And I did. That space gave me a sense of possibility, an idea of the shape my life could take.

Did I begin to imagine sexuality in the same way? True, it was only a touch away, yet my imagination was shaped by sight as much as by thought, as much by the visual media as the written ones. Eventually, as with most of us, sighted or not, it was influenced by touch and by experience both visual and nonvisual, real and imaginary, all intermingled. In the years of my childhood, sexuality was not graphically depicted and was still considered private, if not secret. A Macy's ad for women's lingerie in today's newspaper would have been considered pornographic when I was a child.

Touch is still controlled in a way that vision is not, at least in modern Western societies. The viewer is considered to be innocently exercising individual rights. Looking can be publicly and privately promiscuous and intrusive with impunity. As Jesse pointed out to me long ago, touch in public is pornographic, whereas looking is not. That is the law. At the Mitchell Brothers Theater in the Tenderloin section of San Francisco, which he frequented in his early years, Jesse learned that touching a performer can get even a blind man arrested, just as parking illegally in Berkeley can. Certain laws do not discriminate and are not to be broken, even by the blind.

Embedded in this democratic principle is a certain visual prerogative.

Touch has an immediacy that vision can deny. It does not reside in the equivalent of a kinesthetic blind spot. The touch that is forbidden denied Jesse just as it educated Samantha. This aspect of her education was neither visual nor theoretical, but came to determine her sexual proclivities as much as her nerve endings did. In fact, it educated her naive neurons into an entire way of life. Perhaps it is even responsible for her skills as a sex therapist.

Lacking the subtle morphing of visual cues, the nervous systems and preferences of Samantha, Jesse, Andrea, and Isabel had to be based in literal translation. These nonsighted individuals are, of necessity, practitioners of reductionism. How can they not be? They could try to resist sighted demands and decline each of their performances of sexuality and gender. They could question racializing instead of recoding it to suit their own senses. By why should this burden fall to them any more than to the sighted? They are just trying to get by, to fit in. Who can blame them?

Yet these blind people all reach not for the experience of sight so much as access to the information that comes to sighted eyes, often uninvited. Lacking sight, their goal has morphed into as seamless a performance of sight as possible. In this way, they organize their experience as compensation for a loss that cannot be compensated. The price for this acquiescence to the visual trickster is a high one. It is the loss of self, of possibility, of their own experience, which is replaced instead by proscription and prescription. But who among us, sighted or not, does not yield in some degree to this compromise between desire, discovery and the defined demands of reality?

Is Samantha right that viewing is masculine and being viewed feminine? Yes and no. I myself have made this point in some of my early writing, but Samantha can never know how intrusive sight may be if used in a certain way. The cultural gaze with which she tries to comply is a masculine one; it evaluates appearance and sexiness almost exclusively in women. In recent years, many women have developed a parallel strategy, aptly named "girl power," that I understand as the right to behave sexually as men traditionally have. It is related to Samantha's own strategy not by sight, but by sexuality. However, she lacks the actual experience, possesses only the theory.

You would sound just a little harsh telling someone in public to stop looking at you, although it is done in my native New York, where a certain attitude is normative. "Why don't you take a picture? It lasts longer." And again, unlike the years of my youth, people now do so with the aid of the ubiquitous cell phone camera. Vision has become even more intrusive as these devices extend it to any viewer of YouTube. The sighted can possibly attempt to resist these intrusions. How can the nonsighted? How can they even know what they are missing?

It occurs to me that both Isabel's and Samantha's theories of sexuality and sexual orientation are necessarily reductionist, based in their concrete understanding of such characteristics as clothing and hairstyle. Samantha chooses a decorative form of femininity, Isabel a more stark and unadorned way to signal nonfemininity, which she equates with being lesbian. Samantha and Isabel do not have the sight-based knowledge of movement, body language, and subtlety of facial expression. They cannot practice eye contact, glancing or gazing, staring, or a "come hither" look. They must replace looking entirely with looks rather than indulging in the sighted amalgam

of both. As blind women, they both practice a fundamental form of traditional gender.

Do their strategies work? Samantha's seems to work better, but maybe
she and I are both wrong about this. She appears to have more opportuni-
ties than Isabel does, but several that she is sure were unsolicited. Does she
signal sexual interest in some way that can be mistaken in masculine eyes or
in sighted eyes? Does she have an off switch?

I was the one who was beginning to see more clearly. And what was I
learning so far about sighted codes from dismantling and participating in the
ways that nonsighted people master them? Certainly they were showing me
the encryption code in a way I could never have accessed otherwise. They let
me see the variety of strategies that they themselves used to break that same
code, to understand as best they could and live inside the sighted meanings
of gender, skin color, and sexual orientation. I was far from finished, just
beginning to understand at this point. What could I see with some clarity?

Certainly I could not help but see that vision itself is perhaps the first
human system of knowledge. It is preceded developmentally by touch and,
in sighted development, paired irrevocably with touch, but touch is not a
full language by itself. By the time spoken language is introduced into the
chorus of the senses, seeing is already believing, and the world is well organized. It is so well organized that the very words *I see* have come to mean
"I know something."

And what was I seeing? That the body itself becomes as much a consequence of learned meanings and expectations as of biology or neurology.
Indeed, biology and neurology are developed within an ongoing cultural
conversation. It is the decoding of this conversation to which these nonsighted persons devote themselves. As much as sight is the origin of gendered and racialized perception, it is this very perception that shapes and
educates. The body becomes itself, along with gender, race, and sexual orientation. The human body then is as much an idea as a material reality.

Even in sighted learning, the flux of experience must be organized; the
concrete cannot eternally be poured, but must harden. In this process there
is a fluidity that is lost or hidden, as mattering irrevocably shapes matter.
In this way the human brain invents and learns to see in the very same act.
As the developing brain organizes itself, each person becomes a participating member of the human community. And, forever after, knowledge is as
much an act of memory as of perception.

6

Three's Company

It isn't that they can't see the solution. It is that they can't see the problem.
—G. K. CHESTERTON

LUKE, FLOR, AND LANEY ARE IN their mid-thirties to early forties, Flor being the oldest, and are roommates. In a twenty-first-century update of the television show *Three's Company,* they share a small house in Santa Clara, California, part of the seamless suburban Silicon Valley. Each is, according to the American classification system, of a different race. One is Latina, one African American, and the other Caucasian. That translates into brown, black, and white to the American eye.

What can these designations mean to three blind people? How do their own ideas about themselves as racialized and gendered individuals intersect with each other and with those of their sighted friends and acquaintances? In the recursive interplay of self and society, how does the racialization of American culture affect each of their lives? Can I even tell their intertwined stories without mentioning their particular race? I think not, but let's see how far I can go before it becomes too important to ignore. Or has that already happened?

The similarity with the TV show goes no further than the roommate configuration. Luke, Flor, and Laney are not carefree and hypersexual singles on the prowl for partners in the bars and on the beaches of an always sunny California. All three are single, but not so young and definitely not carefree. What they have in common is that they are blind. This feature complicates their lives enormously, but not in the manner of a sitcom where hilarious predicaments are resolved in a half hour with time-out for commercials. In fact, their situation might make interesting reality TV and is one of the few premises not yet tried in that genre.

Luke comes from a small town in Nevada. He was the only blind child in his class all through school. Yet he had many friends, both boys and girls. From the beginning, he rejected what he calls the "no girls in the clubhouse" mentality. Everyone was "just folks." Was this because he didn't perceive the distinctions? For him there were no differences that made a difference. He was indifferent to skin color and pretty much to gender also. He was a friendly and easygoing boy, appreciative of all the children who approached him. Being blind, of course, he could not approach them himself, for how would he even know that another child was in the vicinity unless that child announced himself or herself in some way?

Luke's mother stayed at home full time and devoted herself to his welfare until she and Luke's father divorced when Luke was about ten. After that, she took a job as a cook in a local diner, but she always saw Luke off in the morning and returned to be with him in the afternoon and evening. He continued to live with her through high school. His father left town and, after one short visit, never saw Luke's mother or their son again. He apparently not only considered Luke's mother his former wife, but Luke his former son; he managed to shed the burden of a blind son along with the wife who had produced him. Soon enough, he left the state and eventually began a new family in rural Missouri. Luke rarely speaks of him, and, when he does, it is not with affection. I can only imagine the despair of a young blind boy abandoned by his father for being, at least in his own mind, exactly what he was.

When Luke and his friends became teenagers, they began to view each other as potential dating partners, and, in that same transformation, Luke lost his egalitarian perspective, as we all inevitably do when desire and preference take over. Yet this is a different kind of discrimination, perhaps a more natural and temporary one. Luke was no different from the other boys in his friendship group. His hormones dragged him right into puberty. He was attracted to girls and not to boys. He mentions this preference only because I ask him directly. I want to know what each of these blind people will say. If there is a deeper and more complex answer, Luke and I do not know each other well enough yet for him to confide in me.

This is not an easy confidence in any circumstance, but, as a therapist, I am more used to hearing it than most. Luke is already different enough from what he wants to be without adding another dimension of difference to his resume. His path would be the straight and narrow, that of unquestioned heterosexuality.

Now his friends were divided along party lines, the girls and the boys. From the boys, Luke sought and received dating advice. He should try to date the more attractive girls, they told him, even though the characteristics that made girls attractive could have no meaning to him. The color of a girl's eyes, the turn of her nose, her smile, her figure had no meaning to him. He could see none of this. Yet he does not talk of developing his own preferences. Instead he followed the advice of his friends to date the kind of girl who would most enhance his status among them. That girl was short and thin with long straight hair. She was white. To this day, this type of woman remains his preference or "ideal," as he puts it. Is he their ideal? He does not say.

Luke's sexual preference is, at least in part, influenced by his male peers and his status in their eyes. And doesn't this happen as well with people who are not blind? This is another interesting question. How many of us are influenced in the choice of a partner by the status that person conveys in the eyes of our friends? I have heard this confession much more frequently from women than from men, although the qualities that women cherish seem to have less to do with physical appearance.

By the time he was ready to be graduated from high school, Luke was also ready to marry one of the girls who fit his friends' description of the ideal. He gained a wife and the respect of his male peers in the very same act. Who knows which was more important to him? Both youngsters were eager to leave the small-town life behind. Perhaps she wanted to see the world and perhaps Luke thought that she would make it possible for him to experience that larger world as well. This is a journey that young people from small towns have been making for as long as there have been cities. The only difference was that these two had only one pair of eyes between them with which to see the outside world. They were young enough and innocent enough to be eager for the adventures that lay beyond their town and beyond their ken.

Luke and his new bride, Francesca, made their way to San Jose, where she began to study nursing at San Jose State University and he enrolled in a training program for the blind. A government stipend would support them. There he learned to work with computers. Although this has been a booming industry in Silicon Valley, Luke has had a lot of difficulty finding and keeping a job. Companies would only hire him for temporary work. He was often unemployed and occupied himself in those times by staying home and drinking beer or smoking pot.

Eventually the marriage came apart under the many stresses of this situation. Luke had to deal every day with blindness; his young wife did not. She saw herself as a caregiver to Luke and, as she said directly to him, she wanted to do nursing as a profession, but not as a lifestyle. Her words stayed with him, and his world collapsed when he felt the sting of that sentence. He had lost his hard-won status, along with the eyes he had married. He was in despair.

Luke was now on his own. He was shocked to be alone; he had never really experienced that before. He was lonely, but worse, he felt like less of a man. Yet Luke has always made friends easily. He is extroverted and tells a good story. In a return to his "just folks" philosophy, he eventually found his two female roommates, Flor and Laney, several years ago. The arrangement has worked well enough for all of them.

Three of my graduate students began meeting with Luke and his roommates. One of the class requirements was that each of the students would establish a reciprocal relationship with one blind person. By reciprocal, we meant that there would be a fair exchange. The student would not exploit the blind person as a subject in a research project, but would try to get to know him or her as a full person and would, in exchange, not hide behind the experimenter's veil of neutrality. They would use a fair share of the time in activities that the blind person chose. In this way, the student would provide a sighted service for at least half the time they spent together. None of the blind people ever refused this offer, and most seized the opportunity to do shopping or errands.

Unfortunately, after an initial burst of enthusiasm, my graduate students found the experience both trying and tedious in much the same fashion that I had at the gallery with Isabel. For example, shopping with Luke began several hours before he and Diane, the student with whom he was paired, left the house. Diane would arrive to find the week's newspapers piled randomly in his room. At Luke's request, they would go through each of the papers and she would describe to him every discount coupon that appeared. He would carefully choose which ones he wanted to use and instruct her to cut them out. And this was only the beginning. At a super-market or discount store, he would ask her to describe what was on the shelves so that he could choose what he wanted.

Here is another interesting perspective on what choice means in today's world of high consumption. Of course, Luke, like most other Americans, wanted this freedom to choose among the multitude of proffered consumer items, but imagine, if you can, going through an entire Walmart doing this. Diane soon developed the same strategy I used; she began to eliminate more and more detail from her descriptions. That worked for a time, but Luke was not satisfied and kept demanding full descriptions. Eventually Diane felt that she could not continue and, like Francesca, she left him.

Diane's experience contributed to my growing understanding of how much information eyes take in and how rapidly and efficiently they do so. So many words and appeals to the other senses are necessary even to approximate the detail and complexity of what a pair of eyes can perceive in a second. My students had expected to be guides, but they were not pre-pared for literal translation any more than I had been.

Perhaps Luke was too angry to compromise or perhaps he had too well developed a sense of entitlement. Perhaps his ideal woman, like his mother, was also meant to take care of him. I was as far from his ideal as possible. Yet I wanted to meet him, to see him for myself, and he readily agreed. We arranged to get together at the house he shared with his roommates.

I would not ordinarily enter a sighted man's room, even on a professional visit. After all, I am not a social worker and I am not a fool. Perhaps I was a bit foolhardy in my decision to visit Luke at home, but I wanted to see how he lived. Nothing about him seemed dangerous or threatening, and I must admit flat out that I reasoned I could overpower or outmaneuver a blind man if necessary. So his blindness altered my own well-crafted gender assumptions even before I met him. Of course, he had never done anything to put Diane in any danger. I was just making the preparations that many women would.

When I arrived at the tract house in the immigrant working-class neighborhood in Santa Clara, I tried ringing the doorbell, but as Luke had warned me, it did not work. Cautiously I opened the front door and called out his name. No answer. Only the sound of heavy metal music emanating from what turned out to be Luke's room. It appeared that no one else was at home. No one responded to my calls. So I followed the sounds of the music and began to knock loudly on Luke's door. It took several knocks to get Luke's attention and then suddenly the music was turned down. For a moment, I felt like the mother of a teenage boy calling him to dinner.

In fact, when he finally opened the door, Luke seemed more like a young boy waiting for his mom than a man in his thirties living on his own. I was taken aback by the mess, particularly in Luke's room, which was littered wall to wall with empty beer bottles, newspapers, CDs, and other forms of chaotic detritus. But for the beer bottles, it felt exactly like the room of an adolescent boy. There were two computers and other assorted technology. In the living room, there were posters and paintings on the walls, but in Luke's room the walls were unadorned. There were no signs of any attempt to decorate or even to clean. A sense of passivity and hopelessness was palpable.

I moved a small mountain of newspapers and tapes and discovered a chair underneath. I didn't wait for an invitation to sit or to engage with him. He seemed so young and so lost that my heart was touched. I said, as warmly as I could, that I was glad to meet him finally after hearing about him from Diane all these months. He gave me very little response, just a gruff and flat acknowledgment. He was not going to be satisfied with a tiny bit of human warmth when he longed for so much more. My practiced therapist's mind began to map out what he needed and how long it might take, how much therapy. It is unlikely that he would ever get that much help though. People at his end of the class hierarchy don't receive individualized and expensive attention. They are more likely to be medicated into a state of quiet desperation.

Yet Luke was generous with his time and his words. I hope I gave him something in return, something more than access to shopping, some sense of mattering. I did come to care for him, but there was little I could do to change his circumstances. Nor could I take care of him in the ways for which he longed. No one could.

A lot of what Luke told me about his life bore great similarity to the stories of the other blind people I had come to know. He was quite depressed and predictably enough had been given medication that was supposed to alter his moods. Also predictably enough, he chose not to take it most of the time and instead used beer for the same medicinal purpose. It is certainly less stigmatizing in this society. A man drinks beer. A mental patient takes medication. And what about the seemingly interminable grief—a grief inevitably tied to a loss? Can that be medicated away?

Belief in medication's effectiveness has been shown to influence that very effectiveness: the best pill is washed down with the elixir of belief. Wanting to "be a man" was so central to Luke's mattering map that his drug of preference was the beer he used for manly medication. Could he even imagine feeling everything the absence of vision meant to him? Could he allow it to matter? And does it matter to anyone but him? While it does matter to me, it is for a mixture of my own purposes and his. I was not ready to see him through the long psychological journey that might replace medication. Neither was anyone else.

So we sat in Luke's room. He drank a beer while I was there. I didn't object. This was not therapy, although many of my colleagues would find it a bit unconventional even with a "research subject." I didn't consider Luke a subject and didn't see any reason to make rules about our interaction unless his or my safety were in question. And they never were. Getting to know him was what I was after, not controlling or changing anything about him. Years of practicing psychotherapy sometimes cause this distinction to blur, but the more I have practiced the more I have come to understand that even therapy is not about change, but instead about giving the person back to herself or himself as fully as possible.

There is a person that each of us might become if that potential is not impeded or distorted by trauma or happenstance. All too common is the sense of learned shame that causes people to hide from themselves and others, to try instead to appear acceptable. For these blind people, so much was wrapped up in passing, in hiding, and in compensating for their perceived defect that they could hardly imagine what kind of life they might have developed without the imperiousness of sight and of the sighted.

But are the sighted performances any less false? Often they are only less clumsy, like the difference between Laurence Olivier and a street mime playing Hamlet. Can any of us be true to ourselves and to the demands of the culture at the same time? How often is this a perfect fit? If it is not, does the culture or the individual suffer the sacrifice?

Unlike the deaf, the blind have not developed their own language or culture. They are often isolated and scattered from each other; they speak their own careful translation of sighted language and seem to have no mother tongue, although I never did come across a nonsighted mother and child.

No wonder so many of them would be alienated from themselves, for that is the essence of the experience society has designed for them. Live once removed from your own experience and instead memorize the words for that of others. And does this not point to how many of the sighted make a similar compromise between self and the many demands of sighted culture, attempting to meet the complex demands of gendered and racialized meanings and the narrow acceptable possibilities of sexual expression. Perhaps the sighted development of self differs only in the seamlessness with which sight permits these characteristics to be interwoven.

Luke actually has quite a bit of ability to move around in the outside world, having learned to use a cane as a young boy. It is not inability that keeps him in his room, but his sense of despair and hopelessness. Like other blind people, he has been taught to pass in the visually centered world. He can move about and dress and act like a man, but is he any more than a reflection that he himself can never see? He lives in the shadows and, in a tragic sense, is one of them.

Luke chooses clothing the same way that Samantha does, via a system of labeling and organization. He prefers to choose by texture, which seems to have more meaning to him than color or pattern, both of which are so central for Isabel. Perhaps concern with color is more feminine. He is trying to be a man. At our first meeting, he is wearing a white T-shirt and black chino pants with an unbuttoned flannel shirt. They are rumpled, as if he gathered them from where they were abandoned on the floor the night before. When I ask him, he does know what he has on, but has no idea of the colors or of the visual impact. He seems not to care very much. Either he is not trying as hard as the other blind people I have come to know to make a certain impression in the sighted world or in his mind that impression has less to do with appearance. His concept of masculinity seems to include a certain casualness about clothing. Possibly his sense of hopelessness has leached all the color from his mattering map. It is too soon for me to know which it is or, more likely, what combination of them all. He does affect a certain nonchalance, as if none of it really matters to him. It is easy to see through this posture right to the heart of how much it does matter.

For now, Luke is ready to go shopping, much as he did with Diane. Today we are heading to Walmart in a strip mall a few miles east. I will help him shop to the extent of my own patience and stamina. I tend to get easily overwhelmed by the endless choices in large stores. I turn away from the experience for which he longs, to be able to look at and touch each item, to choose the items in my life with care. I do not enjoy shopping and tend to be hasty about it. Today I try to slow down as much as possible and to permit Luke the use of my eyes. I think I succeed at this goal enough to satisfy him. We both leave the store with several bundles in tow.

Not today, but soon enough we will get around to talking about what makes a man attractive. Luke is the one to bring it up. He feels that ideally a man should be tall and muscular and definitely good at sports. Like the other blind people I have gotten to know, he seems to have both feet firmly planted on the cultural mattering map of his generation. He knows the theory, but cannot accomplish the practice with any degree of fluency. Luke is tall, but not muscular and definitely not a good athlete. He has some weights in his room, a nod to a goal that he does not meet. He rarely uses them, so they sit there, a reminder of his failure as a man. Perhaps not being able to see them under piles of newspapers and clothing mitigates his disappointment in himself.

Luke says: "I know by touch when I need to shave or get a haircut. As to clothing, I use a system of labeling that was taught to me, but I am lazy about it. If I am dressed wrong for an event, usually someone will tell me. It is hard for me to remember what kind of clothing goes with what kind of event. Sometimes I don't care."

Luke waits for someone else, usually a woman friend or a date, to manage the complex clothing code. I can relate to that. I recall how I disliked opera because I associated the music with the formality and stiffness of the clothing I was required to wear. One day I found myself in what was then East Berlin attending an opera with a friend. Admission was the equivalent of a few dollars in American currency, attire casual and comfortable, and the music entrancing. That evening, opera became about immediate powerful experience rather than a distant performance, and I have retained that relationship ever since despite the difficulty of navigating through a sea of gowns and tuxedos at American opera venues. Is this in any way what Luke feels when he is dressed for a social event?

As I get to know him, Luke continues to strike me as a little boy waiting for his mother to take care of him. I am mindful of the fact that many men transfer this kind of desire from mother to girlfriend or wife. Haven't I written about it in detail in my book *Engendered Lives*? I assume that the kinds of women with whom Luke involves himself take on or have this maternal trait, at least for a time. They also seem to tire of this form of service long before Luke does. In the more traditional marriage, where it may be subtler, this arrangement can last for a lifetime.

I ask Luke what he looks for in a woman.

"I like them to be intelligent," he tells me. "I gave up a long time ago looking for an ideal woman. I don't care at all about hair color. I am more willing to go for convenience."

"And what is convenience?" I ask gently.

"Someone who wants to be with me" comes the all too ready response.

This idea of the ideal haunts me. The desired woman is defined by size, shape, and color. She is as pretty as a picture, one that Luke has never seen. Does she want to be with him? Does she love him? Or does she look good while not loving him? She is elusive, but attractive to his sighted mates, to the cultural eye of the indeterminate observer. With her, he is a man. Without her, he is a lonely little boy.

Luke currently has a sighted girlfriend. His feelings are modulated when he describes her. She is not thin and not considered attractive by his friends. What kind of woman is she? The kind he can get, the best he can do. She is not ideal, but a real flesh-and-blood woman. She does not make a man of him. She does not seem to mind the mess and the sadness of his life; she does not make any attempt to clean and dress him or to take care of him. Perhaps she too needs some caretaking. However, I will not get to meet her and find out for myself, as Luke will tell me soon enough that they have broken up. Even she has left him, perhaps exhausted or perhaps just tired of being found wanting. Perhaps she wants "more of a man."

For now, Luke continues his musings about female attractiveness, with just a bit of prodding on my part.

"I find British and Australian accents attractive," he says. "It might be interesting to be with someone of a different race."

"How so?"

"Just something different, I guess." He does not mention his two roommates, both of different races, but perhaps he is thinking of one of them. Perhaps he says it for my benefit. Perhaps he is exhausted and disappointed by the women he has known and longs for an adventure. Undoubtedly all this and more live inside his simple comment.

"What race would you choose?" I ask. I want his impressions of the differences.

"Maybe a Mexican. I have met so many since I've been in San Jose."

I ignore the common American error of confusing nationality with race. It bothers me, but I will save it for the classroom. For now, I am after something other than educating Luke about the fact that Mexican is not a race or a color. I want to find out what he knows and how he knows it.

"I don't like the sound of the accent and I don't know any Spanish, so she would have to be here long enough to speak pretty good English. They seem kind. They like to take care of a man. And physically most of them are short, which I find somehow attractive. Also the long hair."

This comment spoke for itself at the time as much as it does now on the page. So I moved to the next question on my mind.

"Are there people who offer to help you?"

Luke replies that, when he is outside, there are some who might approach and offer him help.

"Do women approach you? Do men?"

He laughs nervously at the idea that men would approach him, so I try to make the question fit and ask if they hassle him at all. But still he replies that they do not.

"Men never approach me. I do get helped sometimes by grandmother types of women."

How does he know what a grandmother "type" is and whether the woman who approaches fits this model? It is a form of translation with which I have become familiar. He guesses from what clues come his way. He means that he is never approached by a short, thin, long-haired woman looking for a blind man to love.

Luke is a friend of Samantha's, and she has talked to me about him. They did have a brief sexual relationship, but she reports that it was too difficult to pursue anything more seriously as they are both blind and both want to find someone sighted. Yet she speaks of him with warmth and compassion.

"It is much more difficult for a blind man than a blind woman," Samantha tells me.

"There is a standard of masculinity that I just know Luke cannot achieve. On a date, he can't hold the door or order a glass of wine. He can't do the things a man should do."

So they agree on what matters in a man and they also agree just to be friends. What they tell me and themselves is that there was no chemistry between them. When I press Luke a bit on what he understands chemistry to be, he says, "You think about the person and miss her when she's gone." This could describe a caretaker or a friend as easily as it describes chemistry. But maybe it is my idea and not Luke's that these are separate categories.

Luke says that a sighted person has to let him know if a woman is interested in him.

"Flirtation is visual and depends on being able to hold eye contact," he tells me. I have heard these words before and have thought them before. Here they are again. When I first began these conversations, I was not so sure. I did not want it to be the case. By now I sadly agree that the absence of eye contact leaves a gaping space in a relationship. It is not just about flirtation, although it is about that. But it is more, at least for me and the sighted people I know. Eye contact informs every phase of intimacy. It is the channel by which heart connects to heart, soul to soul. I have come to know this in a way that I never would have if I had continued through life looking into the eyes of everyone I met or with whom I developed some intimacy. It has been the startling inability to do so with any of these blind people that has compelled me to experience the importance of eye contact in my own life.

It is the complex and reverberating vortex of sight and meaning, acceptance and desire, interest and connection. I would feel my experience reduced and impoverished without this nexus of meaning and desire. I have become all too aware that I look for the light of connection and recognition, of conversation and friendship, of appreciation and even desire in someone else's eyes. Without having spent these hours with blind people, I never would have known this.

I get to meet Flor, one of Luke's female roommates. The other roommate, Laney, could not make time to talk to me and may not have wanted the kind of scrutiny that she imagined I would impose on her. Flor and I met a few times in the house they share. Our meetings were always in the living room, which was furnished with the kind of old overstuffed furniture that one finds in thrift shops. It was clean and comfortable, with worn flower print fabrics. Of course, lack of funds is not the only factor that leads the way to this furniture; the lack of sight on which such aesthetic decisions are based also plays a part. As much as they care about gender and ethnicity, these roommates seem not at all bothered by the ordinary issue of decor. Faded flowers are the least of their concerns. How would they even know what faded looks like? I have learned my lesson and no longer try to explain such things.

Flor is another kind of flower, the female variety. She is in her mid-forties and was born in El Salvador, but has been in the United States for the past twenty years. Although she is not a citizen, she does have a green card and is here legally, having been granted amnesty and protective status by the U.S. government. She was married to a sighted man who did not have the use of his legs. They lived in the Midwest and had two children. Her son Alberto and daughter Carmen both stayed in Dayton, Ohio, where they were raised and where Flor also lived until recently when she decided to come to California "to start a new life." She is in good company in that regard, as so many of us have successfully done the same. Once her children were grown and on their own, she decided to set out for greener pastures. Her husband had died by that time. She found her way to northern California, where the pastures are a wheat-field brown for a good part of the year, but in every other way greener than those of her Midwestern home.

Flor is still comparatively new in town and, as a result, has not yet found work as a social worker, a field in which she has an advanced degree. In the interim, she has held a variety of lower-paying jobs. She is happy to be in California and very much enjoys the communal living arrangement, which provides, among other things, daily social contact. Flor knows few other people in the area, but she is friendly, outgoing, and eager to meet new people. It is just a matter of time.

Many people have offered her the unsolicited opinion that her children should be taking care of her.

"But I'm the parent," she tells me. She wants to be on her own and has no doubt, after raising two children mostly by herself, that she can do it. Meanwhile, she is still a "parent," as she does most of the cleaning and housework for herself and for Luke. Is this a parent or a wife? I wish I knew the answer.

The cooking includes complex preparations for adhering to and breaking her perpetual diet. Like so many women today, she aspires to be thin and is always on some sort of diet. This cultural imperative has filtered into her psyche via hearsay. I am close to despair from having heard this contemporary feminine ideal repeated over and over by blind women and men. In fact, among them it is even more blatant and concrete than in the sighted world, as it is learned secondhand and with a certain abstract theory or flexibility. It is not directed by the mirror or by the scale, but by the word.

I have become accustomed by now to the very physical sense of disappointment that clutches me by the throat every time I hear one of these gender imperatives translated for the blind. I had so hoped that theirs would be a different viewpoint. Not that I was naive enough to think that I would not find hierarchies and the points of discrimination that seem to be so close to human nature, but I had hoped and expected that they would be their own. Instead these blind people are schooled even more strictly in sighted preferences. Here it is again. How many descriptions of diets and how many preferences for thin female bodies will I have to endure in this lifetime? I choke on the thought in my own form of conceptual bulimia. I wish I could purge myself and, yes, all of us of this crippling obsession. I have certainly reached for that goal over and over again in my work and in my writing, but my reach does not extend far enough to alter a cultural imperative.

Flor tried unsuccessfully to work as a journalist when she was a younger woman. Writing was her first love, but it did not return her deep affection. Traditional journalism demands sight so that scenes are set visually as a context for the imagination of the sighted reader. Flor found a job with a local newspaper, but when she tried to create an auditory context for her reports, her editors found them odd, discordant. She was not appreciated, not published, and eventually let go. At the time, there were no alternatives for the blind, such as the Web sites and blogs that have since flourished on the Internet—although even these are rarely financially remunerative. So, to support herself and her children, Flor turned to a profession not so dependent on visual detail. She became a social worker, specializing in work with young patients diagnosed as schizophrenic by their sighted psychologists and psychiatrists.

Diagnosing mental illness is so tricky a culturally based skill that I cannot imagine a blind clinician practicing this nuanced art. It requires attention to facial expression, eye contact, physical mannerisms, and even manner of dress. The presence of tics and atavisms may help define or distinguish related diagnostic categories. I think of Jesse, running his adolescent groups with a sighted cotherapist simply to make sure that everyone was awake. Flor, however, was not involved in diagnosis or treatment. Since she had to work with clients sight unseen, she was channeled into a job dispensing welfare-related services to a Spanish-speaking group. She did not have to see them, but only to hear them speaking their native language, which was also her own.

As an immigrant, Flor tends to categorize people by their spoken language and country of origin rather than by race. They are Americans or immigrants, and black or white or even brown skin does not figure easily into the equation. These do not matter to her to the degree that nationality and spoken language do or even as much as they do to most sighted people in her native El Salvador. She and I easily speak English and Spanish interchangeably, as is the custom of many longtime Latin American residents of the United States. I am accustomed to this mixture, which is dubbed Spanglish by those who do not speak it but are amused by it.

In this way, I get a small glimpse of a different map. I can enter the world of Flor's childhood in El Salvador with her. She explains to me that, in her village, blindness was considered a curse from the gods. Parents tried to hide a blind child, and Flor went to live in a neighboring village with her grandmother, who trained her to clean and cook but did not allow her to go to school. When she was sent on an errand, the neighborhood children would taunt her, calling her a child of the devil, *hija del diablo*. They would throw rocks at her and trip her. Once someone even spat at her. Although she cannot report this aspect to me, I can imagine the adults standing behind these children and crossing themselves.

When the ravages of war in their native country presented her parents with the opportunity to emigrate to the United States, they were fortunately able to include Flor and her grandmother in their plans. Flor was a teenager by this time. They found themselves, in a matter of hours, transported from their hot, steamy home in El Salvador to an inhospitable Ohio winter, where, after factoring in the ubiquitous Midwestern wind chill, temperatures were below zero degrees Fahrenheit. The sponsoring agency provided Salvadoran families with housing, heat, food stamps, and worn but serviceable secondhand overcoats. Nevertheless, they all shivered through their first Midwestern winter, much as I myself did when I was a graduate student in Columbus, Ohio. Even I felt the cultural disorientation of a displaced New Yorker, which can't begin to compare with what Flor and her family felt that first American winter. Yet the visual impact of the flat and dismal Midwestern landscape did not depress Flor as it did me. Perhaps her winter coat and her return to her parents provided sufficient warmth and comfort to her.

Springtime brought work for her parents and school for her and her siblings. Flor had never attended school before, as there had been no facilities for the blind in her native pueblo. Her parents were hesitant about this opportunity, but Flor was not. She was eager to learn, and the social workers assigned to her family were insistent on her right to an education. Flor was enrolled in a school for blind children. At first, the plan seemed doomed, as she had no formal education and spoke no English. It looked like she was headed for yet more training in the indelicate feminine arts of cleaning and cooking.

But something surprising occurred in time to alter this plan. Flor began to learn English, as well as to read American Braille. In her native pueblo, blindness had been mistaken for intellectual disability, and no one had ever tried to teach her or to help train her mind. Her family was skeptical, but her teachers, at first hesitant, became enthusiastic and supportive. As she learned to speak English, she was able to communicate with the other blind students.

Flor soon made her first friend, a girl two years younger than her, but in the same grade. Flor and Elia now studied together and played together during recess. They were best friends. And, with this, Flor began to thrive, to make more friends, and to speak English and read Braille. In her own way, she was a Salvadoran Helen Keller, and her teachers could not have been more thrilled. Eventually Flor became fluent enough in the English language to prepare herself to become a journalist.

I have read some of her articles, and she is a good writer in both languages. She is fluent and smart, but not able to describe the visual impact of a situation, customary to sighted readers of the news. However, by virtue of her intelligence and her bilingual skills, she was able to succeed in social work, which saved her life. It was a sad decision for her in one way, but homage to her teachers and an expression of gratitude for the life she had been given. Flor is a blind woman who can see an opportunity and wastes little time lamenting her losses. If her milk is spilled, she cleans it up and carries on.

It was while doing that very social work that Flor met Alberto, who eventually became her husband and the father of her two children. Alberto had been born in Nicaragua, and, although he had also lived in Ohio for many years, he had never attended school or learned English. He was sighted, but had an advanced case of multiple sclerosis and was unable to stand or walk without assistance. He was, however, able to give her two children in short order. Their son carries his name. The family stayed together for almost ten years, by which time his condition had grown so severe that he had to be institutionalized. Flor raised their children in his absence, and he died a couple of years later.

This conversation about Alberto and their marriage provides an easy transition to the subject of gender and also of sex, in the conspiratorial way that women friends often confide in each other. Flor opens the topic, telling me about her relationships since having been with Alberto. She prefers attractive men "because they are more confident" and she likes men who have a thin, firm body.

"A fat man does not take good care of himself," she continues in a slightly defensive and scornful explanation. Here again is the preference of the sighted American culture in which Flor resides and which resides simultaneously in her.

She goes on.

"I am also attracted to a good sense of humor and to red hair."

"Red hair?" I respond, more than a little surprised. "It sparkles," she imagines. Someone sighted has explained sparkling to her.

"Men with red hair have witty and vibrant personalities. They sparkle like their hair." Next comes the disclosure that I have heard from almost every woman I have known.

"I try to watch my weight so that I can get this kind of man." Obviously she has known one or two with red hair or "red hair personality."

Flor continues easily and conspiratorially.

"Men perceive blind women as asexual, so you have to work harder to let them know you are interested." If she knew what a wink was, that would be the precise moment to use one. Nevertheless, I feel the psychological wink between us.

"Blind women," she goes on, "are not taught how to be attractive. They are rarely considered to be competition by other women. But I am different. My mother taught me how to be attractive and also how to please a man." Another psychological wink assures me, if I had any doubt, that she really does know.

I must admit that I did not venture to ask her if she had ever been attracted to a woman. I felt that it was too much a violation of her cultural location and intense desire to fit in. She would not only never consider it, but I felt that it would destroy our well-developed rapport. I did, however, approach the topic by asking if she knew of any women who were attracted to other women or men to other men. She replied that she had heard of it, but that it was something that happened only in the big cities. She had never known anyone, she said, who engaged in these activities. I left it there.

Flor goes to elaborate lengths to make herself visible to sighted and hopefully red-haired men. If she cannot see them, she is also sure that they will not see her without some extra effort on her part. She wants to be sure that she too "sparkles," although she really doesn't know what the word signifies. Like the other blind people with whom I have spoken, she translates a visual experience into her own and is left with a belief that she understands the visual world. Some of her flirtatiousness and adornment of her body are the identical strategies of a sighted woman in a visual world. She is complying with the laws of gendered attractiveness. Yet there is an added element. She does not quite know when she is being seen, unless there is a response that she can recognize. And so much of the sighted appreciation of attractiveness requires sight to itself be seen. A brief smile, a look in the eye, an appraising glance, a lowering of the eyes, even quickly blushing.

Flor explains to me, for example, that many sighted people think that blind women all look alike. I will hear this from other blind women as I continue these conversations. I assume that it is so for blind men as well, but they do not seem to be approached by strangers as often or discussed by strangers when they are present. It is a common experience for blind women to be approached by a sighted person who mistakes them for another blind woman they know. Again gendered sight wins the day.

Flor tells me that people often talk about her in public as if she is not there. I hear this comment repeatedly from blind women. For some unknown reason, many sighted men and women have the idea that blind people, and particularly women, cannot hear them, an odd conflating of the senses. As for the public and often very vocal appraisal of blind women, I think it is an extension of the sighted right of men to appraise women at any time, and more vocally when there is a sense of entitlement involved. There is a similar sighted sense of entitlement, of centrality, of the feeling that this person exists by virtue of her effect on me. This is not at all different from what Flor reports. She is visible if she has an impact on her sighted surroundings.

Yet Flor participates in the denial of her own reality by the extent to which she tries to pass in the sighted world. She has been taught, like most educated blind people, to look like she is making "eye contact." Jesse first alerted me to this strategy, and Isabel later called it a good trick. And it is a good trick, the trick of passing that has also been used by gay people, by light-skinned blacks, and by certain Jews. For American blacks, there is a pattern of speech that must disappear along with skin color and facial features. For many Jewish children, especially during the Holocaust, naturally or artificially lightened hair was the key. Later, surgical techniques to alter Semitic features were added to the arsenal. For blind people, it is the illusion of eye contact where there is none. It took me several hours of this experience to train my own eyes in the opposite direction, to be able to look away without discomfort. And still, after years of this experience, it is not easy and feels more like tearing myself away than simply looking away. It has never become casual.

In one of our conversations Flor describes a job interview to me by saying, "the two interviewers looked me straight in the eye." Another time, talking about flirting, she comments, "You should have seen the look on his face." I can only think, although I do not say it, "*You* should have seen the look on his face."

Like most of the other blind people I have come to know, Flor uses sighted language in order to fit in. She wants desperately to be a part of the sighted world. She explains to me that "sight" is a third language that she speaks fluently. How odd would she sound to the sighted world if she were to eliminate all references to sight from her speech? No more "Look at that," "I'll see you later," "I see," "See ya."

It is not just the language; in fact, Flor is extremely interested in what other people look like. She often asks me to translate for her. My descriptions do not produce visual images in her mind. Her brain has not developed a visual area, and, as is so for most blind people, it has assigned other tasks to the visual cortex, typically to process the touch involved in reading Braille. For such a brain, vision becomes located in the fingertips and appearance in the nonvisual imagination (Kaschak 2011).

Flor speaks to me of travel. She would like to visit Hong Kong some day to "take in the sights." I gasp internally. What sights? I continue to be amazed at this blind woman's desire to live in the sighted world as an equal. I am still surprised by this orientation in every one of the blind people I have met. Do they have a social movement or a revolution coming in the future such as those that moved many Jews, blacks, and gays beyond this stage? I cannot say, and I certainly couldn't find or even plant the seeds. Yet visual orientation is as important to them as sexual orientation has been in twentieth- and twenty-first-century Western cultures. In their world, it is of paramount importance to know a person's visual orientation. It defines that individual as much as being gay or black or a Jew still does in the mirror world in which passing is also a temptation.

With both Luke and Flor, there was another interesting visual element in play. My student Janine, who worked with Flor before I entered the picture, was what visual, racializing society names black. So Janine was faced, for the first time in her life, with a struggle about whether to "come out" or not and, if so, how to do it. Janine is not someone who could pass as white in the sighted world, so in her ordinary life there was no temptation for her to do this. No one with two eyes trained to racialize skin tone and facial features would mistake her for white. Of course, no one with two eyes unracialized would ever call her black either, as her skin is a dark brown coffee color that, if anything, reveals the racial mixture of most Americans labeled as black. Yet this assignment is not decided proportionally or scientifically, but rather in the ancient arena of inherited prejudice.

Janine's speech does not bear even a trace of any inflection or pronunciation that would give away her membership in this racialized category. She does not conform to the requirements of cultural synesthesia upon which so many blind people and many sighted ones depend. She does not "sound" black. As a result, Janine agonized over whether to tell Luke and Flor, and what it was she would be telling them. None of the white-skinned subjects had felt the need to reveal their racial group membership, which both they and the blind took for granted as the default position, the "I am white unless I tell you otherwise" position, which itself can contribute to passing.

Janine and I discussed the options, but I did not push her to make a decision. I was as interested in her reactions to this dilemma as I was in the two blind participants. I was interested in the struggle this circumstance aroused in her, and so was she. It was the first opportunity she had ever had to step out of her socially assigned category, and it was not a simple choice for her. Was there a truth that she was denying? Was she ashamed of her designation? Was she proud of it? Did it have to matter so much? Was it even possible for it not to matter at all? Was she lying to herself? To Flor and Luke? It is never a simple choice to betray oneself in order to rescue or protect oneself. Sometimes, however, the illusion of safety is all that is within reach.

For a long time, Janine did not reveal anything to Luke or Flor. With my encouragement, she paid attention to her own experience instead. She told me she felt a little fraudulent, as if she were trying to pass. And in a way she was, in the more traditional manner not of a blind person but of a black woman in contemporary America, where skin color and racial designation are considered immutable. In another tradition, that of light-skinned individuals of mixed racial heritage who are still designated as black, she was able to pass into the dominant racialized group. In a sighted world, Janine's skin was too dark for her ever to have seriously considered this option. It is not that she told Flor and Luke that she was not white; she simply assumed the default position along with them.

Janine began to become aware of a sense of embodied shame just beneath conscious experience with which she had lived unknowingly. The hypervisibility of her black and female body defined her in public without words and almost as readily in more private situations. There was no privacy, no ability to define her boundaries. Her appearance defines her in the eyes of others, of the indeterminate cultural observer, and so ultimately in her own eyes. This was the first opportunity in her life to consider redefining herself, yet both options left her feeling ashamed. How could she deny her heritage? How could she accept it?

Janine felt a sense of relief at not instantly being seen as a black person, although her voice readily identified her as a woman. I don't know if Janine would have felt relieved or disoriented to stand outside both categories. In fact, I'm not sure how I would feel in her position. I can only imagine it as a free fall with nothing to stop me from hitting the ground but the arbitrariness of a vision-based framework. Perhaps this experience would be more stimulating for those who enjoy an adrenaline rush. I suppose that the limit of Janine's own learned and embodied cultural identity had to serve as her parachute. Her very same body demanded a soft landing, as the identity of a black woman in twenty-first-century United States both limits and embraces at the same time.

Janine has lived a lifetime being identified as a black woman, with all its multiple meanings, embedded in her sense of self, her psyche, and her body. She has her family and her husband. Could she deny them and herself for a social experiment? For Janine, this was only an experiment, as she is only visiting the unsighted world. She cannot discard her identity like yesterday's attire.

This unexpected aspect of our experiment highlights the meaning of meaning. Janine eventually decided not to tell Flor and Luke that she was black. I don't know how much it would have mattered to them, but I doubt that they would have told her. My guess is that they would have suffered the humiliation that accompanies their blindness, the inability to acquire direct knowledge of what matters so much in the sighted world. In part, she wanted to spare them this emotion and, in part, she wanted to spare herself. I hope that what she learned surpassed her startled awareness of the extent of pride/shame and embodied vulnerability embedded in her identification as a black person.

When Barack Obama ran for president of the United States, there was some discussion about whether he was "black enough." He is clearly considered a black man, although his mother was designated white. In racialized America, the one-drop determination still holds, and someone with only 1 percent of blood inheritance from a black person is either black or passing. In visually based America, the meanings are developed and decided even for those who cannot participate in the decision.

Luke did not perceive gender until other boys called his attention to it. Although he began to notice girls, it was mostly in ways that would enhance his masculinity in the eyes of his peers. Is this merely an aspect of heterosexuality, or is it a sine qua non? The educational system for the blind has actually been called to task for not emphasizing and teaching heterosexuality clearly enough; most blind schools now include it in the formal curriculum. All other schools carry it as a major in the informal curriculum from the first to the last moments of education.

The division of individuals according to whom they have sex with is yet another cultural question, another *or*. A third category, named *bisexuality*, does not begin to resolve this dilemma but serves instead to bolster the illusion of dichotomy. Before the nineteenth century these categories were not regularly invoked either in Europe or in the United States and are still not used in this way in many cultures. For the nonsighted, the badges of membership must be learned and earned. Is this not so for the sighted as well?

Can Flor or Samantha perform femininity better than Luke can masculinity? They both agreed that they could, but where did they get that idea? Neither the idea nor the decision rests with them. The indeterminate observer is watching them, haunting the eye/mind/hearts of the sighted and the mind/hearts of the nonsighted.

More than any other sense, the eye objectifies and defines. Just as it can invoke intimacy, it can set us at a distance from one another and it can maintain that distance. In twenty-first-century Western culture, the predominance of sight over smell, taste, touch, and hearing has resulted in an impoverishment of bodily relations (Irigaray 1978). Gender and sexuality, along with racialization, are coming to seem to me more and more to be a form of hallucination, not solely but largely visual, that come to shape the human psyche and the human flesh. Is my body, Samantha's or Luke's, Jesse's or Isabel's, a thing or an idea? These questions with an *or* dipped in the waters of meaning are deceptive. A single *or* actually propels us in endless circles, even in conceptual waters. While generations of philosophers and observers have asked this question about the human condition, my answer is my own: both and neither are the case. Mattering is everywhere implicated where there is and is not matter. And, as we are coming to see, so is vision.

7

Talking Black

To see what is in front of one's nose needs a constant struggle.

—GEORGE ORWELL

JANINE'S EXPERIENCE WITH LUKE AND FLOR was about to be reflected in another series of seemingly recursive cultural mirrors. One of my students, Adrian, contracted the flu in the early days of this project. As a result, he spoke with Sonia several times by telephone before meeting her in person. In the familiar pattern of cultural synesthesia, Sonia "sounded black." Based on their telephone conversations, Adrian instantly and without conscious thought assumed that she was a black woman. This reaction is common enough to be readily recognizable to sighted telephone users and is also, in fact, the very manner in which blind people attempt to enter into the sighted code. By the encrypted rules, black is not just a skin color; it is a voice intonation, a particular manner of speech and pronunciation.

Although Sonia may sound black to the racialized American ear, she is not. Her voice and manner of speaking English are what are considered black, while her skin is a color that would be named white. Both are colored differently by the acculturated human mind, but both are colored. Sonia's skin color and her speech patterns do not match as they should according to this system. This discrepancy boggles the racialized American mind. "How did she learn to speak this way and why would she continue?" is the likely question. Her skin color is, of course, immutable. "Isn't she aware that it is a huge cultural disadvantage, or is it a real or perceived advantage in her own largely black community? What can she be thinking?"

Sonia belongs to a Pentecostal church, most of whose members are black, and she has perhaps adopted the speech patterns that she hears every day. Or maybe she learned them as a child and, as a result, gravitated to and was embraced by this Pentecostal community. She does not know the answer to this question, and so neither do I. To my ear, the speech patterns sound well ingrained and are probably a result of early learning. Sonia has no recollections of being around black people as a child, but would she know if she had been? Possibly. Even probably. But not definitely, as Sonia has been blind since birth. Surely someone should have taught her the sighted code, but apparently no one did. As Isabel's house is not the color that she had been told, neither is Sonia's voice.

When I finally meet her, I find Sonia congenial and easy in manner. She is in her mid-thirties, short and round physically, friendly and extroverted psychologically. Her skin is the color that society names white, her hair medium length, light brown, and unkempt, even scraggly. She was born blind, although it took a few months for the doctors and her parents to realize it. She lives this congenital legacy, along with looking white and sounding black. As skin color easily trumps voice, she is white in the sighted world. Is she black in the blind one? She undoubtedly would be if the blind were not so eager to heed sighted authority. If they were not, she would actually be no color at all.

I ask her about the contrast between her voice and skin. Of course, she has never seen her own skin, but has been told that it is white. As an actual color, that description has no meaning to her at all. To the sighted person who gave her this information, a pinkish yellow hue is seen as white through the eyes of the indeterminate cultural observer. So Sonia is named white. Can she decline this aspect of privilege and demand residency in the nonsighted world? Yet even those citizens work overtime to master the dubious art of color coding human life. She lives most of her social life among sighted black people, but continues to identify herself as white. They also see her as white, and she know this because other sighted people have told her so. Sonia is definitely white, a designation that has, at the same time, deep meaning and no meaning at all to her.

She has come to believe—and who am I to say that she's wrong?—that being white provides her with an advantage in the mating game.

And what a game it is. Like the other blind people I have come to know, she hopes to find a partner who is sighted. Sonia tells me bluntly that marrying a blind person would be settling for less; she is telling me that she herself is less than a sighted person. Luckily for her, as a white person, she is more. She hopes to capitalize on these inequities in the marriage marketplace.

"But why would she speak like a black person? How does this aid in her efforts?" I wonder to myself. Perhaps I am attributing too much choice in the matter, and she speaks the way she learned to speak. Elocution lessons may not be in the cards.

Sonia continues our discussion of the mating game. She derides the men she attracts, calling them losers.

"Either they can do no better or they like having someone dependent upon them," she explains to me with a palpable resentment. She tells me of a former friend of hers who was stealing her boyfriend right in front of her, in plain sight, and she did not know.

"Apparently her friends are losers too," I think in my own quick judgment. Yet how could she have known or seen the flirtation going on in plain sight? Who knows what else they were doing that she could not see?

Sonia is very talkative and, as she picks up speed in our conversation, she bombards me with words. I'm sure it is protective for her, but this barrage hits me like an unanticipated hurricane. It shouts in my face, "I am here." Sonia is here, there, and everywhere in conversation. And this unchecked stream of sound can't possibly permit her a nuanced development of abilities that might help her make sense of her physical or psychological environment. All that talking cries out for attention, but of a kind that disrupts rather than connects, pushes rather than pulls. Nor does it allow her to pay equivalent attention to the other participant in the "conversation." I soon begin to grow exhausted. If I am already tired, I can only imagine how she must be exhausting herself. What had seemed merely friendly steadily takes on an air of noisy desperation.

Of course, Sonia cannot see my facial expression or body language and cannot depend at all on what is in "plain sight." Her strategy is to fill up the air around her with words, trying to create a kind of space bubble, as people with sight do in other ways. Without sight, she cannot see the subtleties of its effect, cannot notice that her words, probably developed to protect and connect, soon become just the opposite, as their hurricane force prevents any approach or response. I feel the urge to back away from her. Suddenly I am a bit less judging of her former friends.

At lunch, I experience more about Sonia than her words. As we eat our sandwiches, my eyes are assaulted by her "table manners," a phrase I have not heard since my own childhood and adolescence. I hear my own belea-guered mother reminding me not to eat with my elbows on the table. I never did learn this. I was something of a socialization failure, and I still put my elbows improperly on the table when I eat. Is this retained habit a bit of defiance or just for the comfort of my body and enjoyment of my food? My mother certainly had gender in mind in this admonition, and I just as certainly failed the test.

Sonia has failed not only "White Speech" but also "Table Manners 101." I keep my eyes on my sandwich, but a horrified fascination draws them irre-sistibly back to Sonia, who is tearing off large mouthfuls of roast beef and chewing them loudly and enthusiastically. Her mouth is wide open. I am fascinated by this spectacle and cannot force myself to look away, much like a bystander at a train wreck. She seems to be enjoying her meal, but I am not enjoying mine. In fact, I am struggling to get through it. Sonia's manner has the air of untamed indulgence. I find my own sight a disability in this circumstance, as I cannot bear to look at her or to look away. As her speech patterns are wrong for her skin color, so is her manner of taking in food completely wrong for her gender.

Sonia definitely has her wires crossed. She has not been trained to eat with proper manners or else she has failed the course. Were she a man, she might have passed with a C-, as more of this behavior is permitted to the gender that is not hers. This lack of containment is very unfeminine. What kind of man wants that kind of woman? What sighted person wants to look at the chewed food inside her mouth as she speaks? In the sighted world lips are the border between ordinary food and disgust. Food once chewed is no longer just food, but takes up internal corporeal residence. This distinction is said to be built into our sight and our minds as humans, an evolutionary protection perhaps against contamination. It has been refined in twenty-first-century America, and more so for women. While gendered demands are modified by class and other group memberships, Sonia is far beyond the pale in any cultural group, except perhaps the blind. She has not been properly socialized to the sighted world where she hopes to reside with the aid of a sighted partner. I am thinking that she will never make it to full residency without a greater attempt at assimilation. She is too much of a foreigner.

On the same days that I meet with Sonia, I have also arranged to meet with Susanne. I want to make a comparison between them, and the juxtaposition in time aids me. Sometimes these dates are an hour apart, and only rarely on consecutive days. The closeness helps focus my eyes on commonality and on difference. Susanne is a tall woman. She is slender. She is black. She knows it because she has been told so repeatedly all her life. She has never looked in the mirror or even looked down at her own body. Although she is blind, her skin, invisible to her, is obvious to the sighted. She is everything that Sonia is not.

Susanne's teachers and parents trained her carefully in femininity. They admonished her regularly not to sit with her dress up or her legs apart. If she was talking too loudly, they told her to quiet down and contain herself. When she developed to her full height of just under six feet by age eleven, they said that was unfortunate. She figured out for herself that it was better to be sighted than blind in a sighted world. She figured out with all the help that we all get that it is better to be white in a world that judges and treats black people as black people and white-skinned people as generic people. Susanne does not sound black. Her manner of speaking English would not give her away. Her skin does. Yet they are both given away every lived moment of every day.

Susanne remembers her first boyfriend, in sixth grade, for many reasons, but especially because he was white and he was, of course, shorter than she was. I recall that at that age most boys are still shorter than many girls and have a later growth spurt in junior high school. I remember the hormone-induced changes in the boys at my junior high, the cracking voices, increased height, and sometimes uncontrollable erections as they stood in front of the class giving reports. Eddie, my own first boyfriend in sixth grade, was also shorter than I was, and I soon threw him over for the taller, handsomer Louis. It was a coup as much as it was a romance, especially in the eyes of my girlfriends. Yet I was not compelled to consider the visual abilities or skin color of these two boys; to the cultural eye, it was exactly the same as my own. I know now that a painter with a trained eye would differ strenuously, but we were not painters. We were children learning culture every day just as surely as we learned long division.

Susanne also recalls, as I do, that at that age the girls were more concerned with fitting in and making themselves acceptable in the eyes of the boys as

well as the other girls who served as the front-line monitors of appropriate appearance and femininity. She remembers the boys in her group being
much more daring than the girls. For example, they would find ways to get
liquor before they were of age. Gender was everywhere and was of paramount importance. Yet she remembers all too well that the issue of sight
was the most central and the most important on her own mattering map.
She wanted to be as good as sighted people, and so did all her blind friends.
Comparing herself to boys or to white people was never as important and is
still not for her. If she could miraculously see, she would be happy to notice
different skin color and gender-based body language. While these are not
the least of her concerns, they are also not the most important.

Many blind women feel that they have to be exceptional "to catch" a
sighted man. Why do we use these hunting and fishing metaphors for
women "snaring" a man? Whose metaphors are they? Susanne explains that
a blind man can be more ordinary than a blind woman and still attract a
sighted partner. Again I learn that in the blind world it confers high status to have a sighted person interested in you romantically. Susanne repeats
what I have heard so many times before about blind men. They will ask a
sighted friend what a particular woman looks like. Susanne says they are
especially concerned that a woman is thin, and they prefer long hair—just
as I wanted a taller, handsomer, and more intelligent boyfriend when I was
only eleven. Do any of us ever outgrow these induced desires—and at what
cost do we hold onto them?

Susanne attended a school for the blind where there were not many other
black students. I must say that I have begun to feel increasingly awkward
every time I use this sighted reference to categorize people who do not have
sight. The more I write about it, the stranger it feels. It was accepted lore at
Susanne's school that black people had drier skin and a completely different
kind of hair. Susanne recalls vividly that when her hair needed braiding the
school officials would ask the kitchen staff to perform this aspect of black
grooming. A sighted black friend of mine remembers all too well that when
her white mother (yes, she had a white mother, but she is defined culturally and personally by the other parent) took her to get her hair styled as a
child, the stylists in the salon refused the task. While they simply claimed
that they didn't know how to deal with black hair, she remembers the story
decades later and tells it to me with as much shame as indignation. She
felt and still feels the sting of racism, of having black hair in a white world.

In fact, she has her hair straightened to emulate the hair of the other race, although she would never say this. It is just a style.

And, of course, it was not just about hair. The other children were well educated by their parents to think of black people as "lazy, not smart and not particularly clean." These beliefs wounded Susanne every day as much as or more than her blindness did. How many ways would she have to be inferior, be culturally labeled with words that made no sense to her?

And how is it that marginalized people are so readily defined by their perceived deficits while their strengths are ignored? Psychologists and sociologists have considered this question. They have noticed the greater social support in economically impoverished communities, the greater role of organized religion, and the greater ease with body image and puberty among black American teenagers (Simmons and Blyth 1988; Nichter and Vuckovic 1994). Yet this admixture of issues is rarely noted, any more than it is in the disabled. Who asks what strengths develop in the blind? Perhaps it is a foolish question, but it is certainly a reflection of a fixed way of thinking.

How is it that light is privileged over darkness, the sun over the moon, and white over black in so many cultures influenced by our old friend the indeterminate observer? How does he form his and our preferences? We have already considered the invasion of the mind/heart so well accomplished by the acceptance of simplistic dichotomies, black and white thinking, perhaps more accurately black *or* white thinking. The *or*'s continue to misguide the very boat they are designed to steer. Such habits of thinking are not so simply dismissed, but become another form of the long division we are taught more formally in school. Black and white, even in thought, divide us not only from each other but from ourselves.

Susanne tells me that it made her "kind of paranoid," as she realized that sighted people could always see what she was doing, whether eating food or kissing her boyfriend. Of course, she never knows for sure where they are and when they can see her. She has had to memorize the details of this circumstance of visibility.

For example, Susanne and the other nonsighted people I've come to know are all aware that sighted people can see through windows, but not through walls, through the sunlit air, but not so well in the dark. When there is no sunshine to permit sight, they need something called lights in order to see. These imitate the sun's light. The sighted need these lights in their homes and feel at a disadvantage in the homes of the nonsighted if the lights are not turned on. Not only can they not see, but they may feel frightened or endangered, as Samantha had already explained to me. Additionally, some sighted people need to use eyeglasses as a visual aid. These glasses sharpen something called the focus of their eyes. Yet Susanne can only imagine what glasses actually do or what lights are. These visual "facts" must be learned and memorized, but are not as useful to her and certainly not as automatic as they are to the sighted. In fact, they have no meaning to her, even in imagination. How could she imagine lightness and dark, sunlight and electric lamps, skin color, a facial expression or body language, an attractive or unattractive woman or man?

Since my early meetings with Jesse and Isabel, I had been slowly coming to realize that these words have no referents for the nonsighted. I thought they did, and Jesse and Isabel almost convinced me that they did. Jesse, of course, had once had vision and may have been able to call up the experience in his memory. However, even he was not sure, and neurology teaches us that the visual areas of his brain have probably been reassigned other functions by now. Although Isabel insists that she understands colors, and Andrea and Samantha claim they "know" the paintings and pictures on their walls, in fact they do not. The sighted world exists only in their imaginations, and I was only a visitor in that territory. I wondered how Susanne could seek privacy and feel too visible. Isabel often spoke to me about "feeling invisible" on the streets of Berkeley. Did they feel something, or just memorize something else? I can never be sure, but I had begun to suspect the latter.

During the same period I was meeting with Sonia and Susanne, I came to know Gilbert, who prefers to be called Gil. He is in his forties and is also black. He works as a counselor in the local Department of Rehabilitation, a career similar to that of Flor. He grew up in Baltimore and, as a boy, was often beaten up by other boys for the crime of having black skin. His blindness did not seem to interfere with this youthful initiation rite. And he learned his lesson well, the lesson of a blind person. That is, he controlled what he could and chose not to be black in the nonsighted world. He accomplished this easily by carefully not "talking black," as he puts it.

As a result, he tells me, Gil sometimes hears racist comments from blind coworkers who do not realize that he is black. He tells me that he has had to endure his coworkers calling a client "a nigger." Gil chose not to comment so as not to reveal his own racial group designation. He exercised the option to keep it invisible, although it is a hollow victory. There is breathtaking loss built right into his meager gain. Yet who am I to question this strategy?

Gil lives inside this dilemma. He tells me frankly that "people don't like blacks and that blacks don't like whites." With little prodding by me, he also produces a variety of other racially based stereotypes, including that Chinese are short and very industrious, whereas Mexicans are short but lazy. While he acknowledges that these are stereotypes, he has not really chosen to question them or challenge them even in his own life. Instead he has committed them to memory and uses them to elevate his own position on the racial hierarchy. This is a strategy not unknown in the sighted world.

Gil is eager to talk about relationships between men and women, and I can by now anticipate many of his comments from the voices of other blind people I have come to know. "A man has a strong and muscular body," he says. Women "always want to look better than they do." He readily tells me he would never go out with a woman who is obese. "Men are more critical, especially about appearance, than women are. A man wants a young and attractive woman." Here it is again; a blind man concerned with a woman's appearance can only be concerned with its meaning in the eyes of the sighted. What else is a woman's appearance to a blind man? Gender and culture trump or, better said, form desire. As Gil works with the disabled, he has also noticed the role of gender. With new clients, he explains to me, the woman partner remains loyal if the man becomes disabled. However, if it is the woman in a (heterosexual) couple who becomes disabled, the male partner often leaves. Gil's explanation is simply that women are "natural" caretakers and men are not. He comments that "men get a lot more than they give."

The conversation turns easily, at this point, to sex between a dating couple. Gil explains to me that before having sex it is necessary to "lay the ground-work," that is, to get to know someone. His idea of an attractive woman is, yet again, someone who is thin and has long, blonde hair. An attractive man is muscular and should never cross his legs. Women have an angular sort of walk, he adds, while men just walk. He confirms what Jesse and Samantha have told me, that both *Playboy* and *Playgirl* are available in Braille and that much of what they know about dating and sex comes from those pages.

Like the other blind people I have met, Gil insists on using visual language. He speaks the language almost fluently. Yet he is talking about sights unseen. He lives in a world where skin has no color at all, yet his world is haunted by the specters of the sighted world. He is seeing ghosts.

8

Double Blind

Here is the shadow of truth, for only the shadow is true.
—ROBERT PENN WARREN

ABIGAIL AND GABRIELLE ARE IDENTICAL TWINS. That is, their lives sprung from a shared group of cells and then developed in the same womb. They share so much, including being blind. Although identical twins have the same DNA and thus have many characteristics in common, the differences in experience and environment make them far from identical. In fact, it has been said that, in the conversation between nature and nurture, the latter has the louder voice (Lipton 2006a, b; Bird 2007; Haque, Gottesman II, and Wong 2009; Jablonka and Raz 2009). There has been nowhere better for scientists to eavesdrop on this conversation than in studying these twin pairs.

Abigail and Gabrielle—or Abby and Gabby, as they are known—live in the Bay area, Gabby in Oakland and her sister in the small rural town of Graton, California, about an hour's drive north of the city. For a psychologist, discovering twins with a similar affliction is like striking gold. We love to study similarities and differences in identical twins who start life with the same genetic makeup. These identical twins are also identically blind not as a result of genetics but as a result of the incubators that blinded so many premature infants of their generation with life-saving oxygen in doses too large to permit development of the eyes. These two tiny twin girls were born early, but healthy. The doctors saved their little lives but destroyed their sight in the process.

I make yet another first phone call. Abby answers. She is in the midst of preparing a meatloaf and describes the messy condition of her hands in enthusiastic and humorous detail. We both laugh and succeed in bridging the gap between us for that moment.

I had hoped to meet with Abby and Gabby at the same time. Although Abby is a musician, she clearly did not inherit her sensitive ear from her mother, who chose these euphonious, almost nursery-rhyme-sounding names for her daughters to carry through life. At any rate, the two don't get together frequently and have decided they need their time together to work with their new dogs and perhaps later on will meet with me. I wanted the opportunity to get to know their relationship, to get to know them together as well as separately. But this is not to be. Despite my initial disappointment, I will soon meet them both and continue my visual/nonvisual education.

On the following Monday afternoon, the last day of August and the hottest day of the year, I set out for Graton. I am to meet with Abby at her home where we will spend the afternoon together. She has, without any hesitation and with well-earned confidence in her ability, given me elaborate and accurate instructions about how to get there. I remember that she took my telephone number instantly, saying she could remember it, just the expectation about which Jesse had admonished me. She is a whiz and wants me to know it.

Abby has been happily married to Zach, a sighted man, for more than ten years. By now, I have been told enough times that it is harder for a blind woman to find a husband than it is for a blind man to find a wife. This piece of information is also evocative of a nursery rhyme, but, at the same time, is not an unexpected corollary of our culture's gender arrangements. Of course, the psychologist in me wonders what they mean by "happy" and what sort of arrangement they have worked out that permits them their happiness. A successful long-term relationship takes a lot of work for any two people, and especially these two, I would think. It may help that they are both musicians—Abby a composer of electronic music, in the tradition of Mort Sobel, and Zach an opera singer—and they share that rich sensory experience.

Abby's directions are perfectly suited for a sighted person, and I arrive easily at the street where she lives. I step out of my air-conditioned car into a blast of August heat that almost knocks me over. Graton is a bit too far to benefit from the cooling summer fog of the San Francisco Bay.

A moment after I ring the doorbell, the front door opens to the eager leap of her new dog, happier to see me than I am to see him. Abby herself also flings herself at me in an awkward embrace. Later I will interpret this premature hug as a way of getting a nonvisual "look" at me, as she doesn't touch me at all for the rest of our time together, even though our conversation is long and intimate.

I try to test myself each time I talk on the phone now to see what kind of visual image my brain has formed of each person, to test how accurately my own mind's eye translates sound. My image of Abby was that she would be very pretty in the way society defines it for a woman. That impression came from hearing her voice on the telephone, its tone and its sense of confidence, of command, the voice of a woman who is used to being admired by men, who commands, not demands, attention. The addition of a sighted husband seems to reinforce that image as it turns itself into an idea. I picture her with long dark hair, not blonde, but otherwise the archetypal Californian. I don't know why I do not see blonde, but she does not sound blonde to me. And she is not. She is also not particularly pretty to the well-socialized eye. Abby's appearance was a product of my learned imagination. I am no different, in this aspect, from Jesse or anyone else who imagines.

Would Abby be pretty in a nonsighted world? Would there be an equivalent for women? As far as I have been able to tell up to now, the gaze of the sighted is the measure of the nonsighted as well. If she is not pretty to the carefully trained cultural eye, then what else is pretty but that?

Abby looks less in command in person than she sounds on the phone and much younger than her forty-eight years. Her movements are stiff, with a staccato sort of rhythm, as she leads me through her home, walking proudly without aid and without touching anything. Abby leads me directly to her music studio and then to her office, where we can talk privately and where she can show me how she works. Her work area is impressive, filled with computers, scanners, and other audio equipment that I cannot begin to identify. She is surrounded by computers that read for her, speak to her, code in Braille for her, and remember her music for her. What technology has made possible is impressive and offers Abby a life that would not be possible otherwise.

She has already mentioned to me in one of our phone conversations that she has a lush, beautiful garden filled with flowers. I am eager to see it and to sit among the flowers and plants on this hot summer day. I too love a beautiful garden, so I am stunned when I finally see this lush paradise. To my eye, the backyard is not quite a garden, and not even a garden that satisfies her nonvisual senses. Anything but lush in my sense of the word, it is a large expanse of bare ground dried by the heat and faded to a cool green with patches of brown interspersed everywhere. Here and there a few lonely-looking shrubs bordered by scattered and scraggly poppies bravely insist upon themselves. Our feet kick up dust as we move through the "garden." Is she wrong or does lush simply mean something different to Abby? Is this barren landscape at the same time wild and lush?

In one sense, Abby's ability to conjure up an image of an unseen garden is equivalent to my ability to create a mental image of her. But I am finally beginning to realize something crucial. I don't know why it took me so long, but it did. Jesse may retain some ability to imagine visually, but Samantha and Isabel were doing something else. If they were deceiving me, they were first and foremost deceiving themselves, especially Isabel, who wanted so much to learn to see. And Abby, who insists upon her own experience, does have a lush garden, even if I cannot see it. Perhaps it is my own eyes that deceive me.

I am repeatedly surprised by how much I count on looking into someone's eyes as I am speaking to them. It has taken me a while to break this habit with these blind people, all trained to maintain what appears to me to be eye contact. The habit is deeply neurological, as primitive parts of my limbic system instruct my visual cortex to look for friendship, danger, or dissimulation in the eyes. When I do so, I find nothing, and it is uncomfortable not to be able to rely on the cues that I know so well. Also I am left with no way to signal my own emotions except with words. As the modifiers of my words are often subtle and not so subtle facial expressions, it makes my own communication more concrete and specific than is usual for me. "Just kidding." How many ways can I say it? Can I ever come close to making my facial expressions intelligible to a blind person?

In the background, the sweet and insistent sound of wind chimes punctuates our talk with a grammatical meter that only the wind understands. We add our voices. As always, I begin by explaining what I am doing and asking for permission to tape our conversation. Abby asks if the transcription is tedious, and I explain that my students are doing it, so it is not so bad for me. Again we are joined together by laughter.

"You know I had a job like that once," Abby tells me.

"When I first started graduate school, I was broke. I had a food budget of ten dollars a week. I learned all kinds of things to do with jello and macaroni and cheese." We both laugh, as I recall that my graduate-student staple was canned franks and beans, with M&Ms for desert.

"It's a lot easier to eat that stuff when you're twenty-two," we agree.

After this student regimen of near starvation, Abby finally got a job at the university taking dictation for a book that a professor was writing.

"One of my best moments was when the professor went to dictate his book one night and fell asleep." We both laugh, I a little more warily than she, as her opening story about a foolish professor does not escape me. I wonder what is coming next and don't have to wait long to find out. She continues.

"Of course he would never admit it, but I had this tape that I turned on that just went zzzzz. So of course I ran and played it for everybody. It was quite a hit."

I am already getting an idea of how Abby negotiates feelings about her blindness. She outsmarts the sighted people whenever possible with her intelligence and her humor. Perhaps she is playing with me too.

Abby goes on to describe other problems with sighted people, especially how much they talk about her in public places, as if she cannot hear or understand. Again there are several stories about how she has outsmarted them. She is certainly both smart and clever enough to accomplish this Pyrrhic victory, but how sad that she feels she must be prepared to do so repeatedly. She is determined to show anyone who questions it that she is as good and as competent as they are. I guess that she wants also to prove this to herself.

"When I applied for graduate school was the first time that I ran into 'We don't want you because you're blind' on such a large scale. I had more rejection letters from graduate schools than you can imagine, from all over the country. Some of them were really blatant about it. Others would just say. 'You're not good enough.' There was a part of me that knew I was good enough because I'd gone to a very good school. I had a 3.9 grade point average. I had won all kinds of awards and competitions and I knew what kinds of schools people around me were getting into. I got to the point that the only good school that hadn't rejected me yet was Ohio State. So I bought a one-way airline ticket, put as much stuff as I could into my backpack, and went there. I didn't know how I was going to pay for it. I didn't know where I was going to live."

Her first semester was rough. When she auditioned for the orchestra, the conductor was impatient and frustrated. The next day, passing an office with an open door, she overheard the orchestra director and a couple of the professors talking about trying to find a way to keep her out of the orchestra, so she stuck her head in and said, "If you are really going to talk about me like that you should close the door lest I come by."

She adds, with a small laugh, "I had to keep doing ornery things like that, but eventually I got the degree that I wanted."

Abby continues with stories on the same point, in which she always emerges triumphant. They have the air of revisionist history with the endings that we humans invent when reviewing a problematic event at 2 A.M. Yet her concern with this theme is more important to me than the literal truth of the events. She is telling me what matters to her and how she would want such events to turn out. Who among us can blame her for wanting to triumph, to have the right bon mot to win the day?

I ask her where she got the idea that she could do what she set out to do so successfully.

"My mom had a lot to do with it. She started the process of showing us how it was going to be out there. 'Face it. You're living in a sighted world. To compete, you've got to be a little better than the next guy or they're going to take the next guy who is easier for them.' She pushed us pretty hard and she really gave us a lot of motivation to figure things out.

"My dad was an alcoholic. And when he finally quit, he didn't use Alcoholics Anonymous or any assistance. He did it by pure stubbornness. And I know I have a certain degree of his stubbornness in me."

Our conversation turns from family to the issue of race.

"Well, you pick up a lot from the sound of things. It's interesting. My sister will have a lot of interesting things to say about race when you meet with her. She just recently came back from Alabama where her husband's family lives. One of the things she said to me was that it's a lot harder when you get down there to tell if somebody is black because everybody has a southern accent. I have never had a situation when I really thought it mattered. Sometimes I would ask Zach later out of curiosity.

"What does a person's race tell you?"

"Nothing really. There are certain kinds of information that you have available to you through your eyes that I have no interest in having because I have no concept of what you are talking about. Like if you started describing to me all the different colors in the sky. I mean I've heard ideas about colors. I'm not ever going to come to you and say, 'Ellyn, what colors do you see out in the sky right now?'"

"So it has no real meaning to you. They are just words."

"Right. And actually I'll be interested in comments like 'Oh, the sky looks like a thunderstorm is coming or the sky looks like it's going to cloud over.' You know, information that tells me something I need to know. Something that really has meaning to me, but not descriptions of sunsets. If somebody is describing something like yellow or blue, I'll kind of form a sense that this is a bright thing. I may wonder if there's a lot of activity. Is this just one color and is it dull or exciting?"

"What would bright or dull mean?"

"I associate them with being exciting or boring. I'm probably picking up more on the emotions of the person describing it to me."

"I wonder if you would try to translate into music or some system that makes sense to you."

"It's funny you ask that because I got a call from a friend of mine who is taking a multimedia class. He came home with an assignment that just blew me away because I think it's an impossible assignment to do. The assignment was to use sound to teach a blind person about color. I said, 'You can't do it because you won't ever know if we got it. Plus it's not even the same from one sighted person to another.'

"One day I bought a dress. I asked every one of my friends individually what color it was and I got completely different answers. So I know it's a subjective kind of thing even among sighted people, let alone trying to explain something of which I have no concept whatsoever. You can't make a sound to mean green because there is green that is a kind of force. There is green that is maybe cool vegetation. I've heard green referred to as a flame coming out of a log. Then there is a green that is all moldy.

"It's something like this table, for instance." Abby places her hands on the table near her chair.

"There is no way that I can form a picture of the table as a whole or, for that matter, of anything that does not involve me. Everything is me. When I think of the table in my mind, it's me touching the table. It's me walking around the table and tracing the table. So when I think of pine green it's either me stepping on pine needles or me hearing the sound or the smell of pine needles. Your body is part of the whole thing. I have no idea of an entire table or of a table separate from my own hands, my own body."

The separation of the sighted is also an illusion. As every agent of culture teaches it, most of us come to believe in our own separation from others and from the environment. Western psychology considers the ability to separate a criterion for mental health. To the sighted human eye, there is only empty space between things. But is the human eye the arbiter of reality, or does it just see what it can see and what it has learned to see?

Our own human disconnection originates in sight. We cannot see atoms, cannot see the activity going on in spaces that look empty to our eyes. Did the severe separation from nature and from others endemic to the West begin with the tyranny of the human eye, which sees separation where there is none?

"It seems to me," I say to Abby, "that a lot of what blind people do is try to speak a second language. You have learned to speak a sighted language almost as if you were bilingual."

"Yeah, and in fact I used to have a lot of fun with people who would be afraid to use words like *Have you seen this movie?*" I acknowledge that when I began talking to blind people I noticed how much that kind of expression occurs in everyday language.

"It feels awkward to use it and also to not use it."

"But what people forget is that we grow up learning the same language. There are certain words that get used among blind people when we have particular topics we discuss that aren't necessarily things we can actually perceive. One of the things that my sister and I got into when we were really little was creating our own language. It's very common for twins to have their own language. We used to get swatted for it too. Neither one of us can remember a whole lot of this anymore, because we were so young when we did it."

"Was it a whole different language, or different words?"

"Oh, it was different words and different sounds. It just grew up between the two of us. We were just great at making up words."

"So nobody else could understand it? Just the two of you?"

"Right."

"And we'd just have our own little codes. It was great fun." I know by now that great fun for Abby means putting one over on sighted people, just like "a neat trick" for Isabel meant faking out the sighted people to believe that she could understand sight. I can understand how much they would want to triumph over a people and a worldview that they cannot share, the impulse for someone who feels "less than" to convince themselves that they are really "more than." Haven't I done this myself? Haven't we all?

I ask Abby if she and her sister had their own concept of the world that they shared only with each other.

"We did. There was a way that the two of us were in our own little circle and then there was the rest of the family just outside us. We'd play with our brothers every once in a while, but for the most part we were pretty much just off, the two of us. Of course, we eventually figured out that our brothers would fight with each other, but we never did."

"My mom said that when we were learning to walk it was really hard for us to let go of something stabilizing and walk into the center of the room. Now I understand her pride in walking without touching anything."

I think about the gender difference, the closeness of twins, and the insulated world of two blind female twins, these two particular ones. Nowhere in the multiple intersections of these realities was there any physical fighting. Not even much disagreement. Perhaps they could not afford to pay the price, but perhaps they also had no need to differentiate themselves from each other, for one to dominate the other, at least at that point in their lives. I wonder how they negotiate the closeness of blind twins with the presence of husbands in adulthood. I file this question away in my mind for future reference. Perhaps I will one day have the opportunity to find out. I still am intent on exploring their blind-together world.

"I'm very interested in this idea of your separate world," I continue. "For example, what if blind people were inventing the world? I imagine they wouldn't invent race, for example, because it's color based."

"Right," says Abby. "But still there are the cultural aspects of history that come with knowing about your ancestors and your family and what they did and your family traditions. I assume that there would still be people everyone is more or less comfortable with—you know, from your own group.

"When we were kids there was an organization that had classes on Saturdays and ran different events. They had a summer camp for us blind kids. I probably met more kids of different races there than anywhere else. And nobody cared. But when we got into adolescence, then problems began cropping up in families because the parents would realize that their white daughter was dating a black guy, for example. Basically the blind kids didn't care."

I tell her that some blind people I've met didn't even know that a person was black until somebody else told them. I add that the blind person saying this was usually, but not always, white.

"That does happen sometimes that you don't know if someone is black or white, but it's no big deal. What you have in common is more important. The thing that was affecting us culturally and influencing us culturally was being blind and that we had the common experience of the stuff that went on through this one organization. That was a strong link, so we had something else that was drawing us together more intensely. Our concern was about being blind or not blind and not about white people and black people."

By high school, Abby tells me, she was involved in the orchestra and other activities that weren't common to most of the blind kids. "So the teachers used to call home and tell my mother I thought I was better than everyone else and I was stuck-up. I wasn't associating with the other blind kids. I don't have to like somebody because they're blind. I don't deliberately dislike someone because they're sighted, but I make my choices based on what I want to do."

"Where was your sister?"

"She was pretty much in the same boat that I was. She wanted to sing in the choir. We would come home at the end of the day and compare notes on what the teachers had done that day. Then she started getting into languages and she found her own little group and escaped too."

"Is that what she wound up doing—languages?"

"She's had several different careers. I was always focused on music."

"You're different that way."

"Yes. And to this day, we just don't like competing against each other. We've actually had some very interesting discussions about what our reaction is if we're in the middle of having some sort of great success and things are not as good for our twin. We try to share our successes as much as possible. It's an old habit."

I ask Abby about dating, and she tells me she and Gabby had one experience that she knows is common to all blind people.

"The first time you start dating a sighted guy you think, 'Why is a sighted guy going to date me? What's wrong with him? Why isn't he getting sighted women?' Yet among the blind community it's quite a status thing to be dating a sighted guy. I actually know, just right off the top of my head, five blind women who are my age who married ten to fifteen years ago right at that age when it felt really important to marry a sighted guy. And they got a jerk."

"How were they jerks—in the same ways or different ways?"

"Oh, lots of different ways. A lot of them were really controlling. Some of them would not allow them to go places, not allow them to be independent. By the time they're all getting to my age, they're saying, 'Wait a minute. What are my priorities? My life is miserable. I don't have to put up with this stuff from another human being.' And they're all getting divorced. Three of them happen to have currently met a blind man and realize that they have given up certain things by finding a blind person, but escaped others."

"So you think that means they've learned to accept something about themselves?"

"Probably. Partly, yes."

This is a "Yes" that screams "No." I think that what they have learned is to reject a strategy that did not work well for them. As to a deeper insight into their own rejection of themselves, I cannot say more than what Abby is telling me, and she is saying "No" in every way but with words. As with any second marriage where the partner is chosen for being different from the first one, there is probably trouble ahead and not much resolution of the issues involved.

"Most of us still believe that the definition of success is to make it in a sighted world and to be one of them." This answers my unspoken question.

"Do you think there's any alternative ideology like, 'Let's make it in our own world?'"

"There are certainly some occupations that are well suited for blind people. So what will often happen is that one blind person will crack an occupation and then, boom, you get an influx of others."

"But not more of a political movement like 'Let's live our own way and not try to be mainstreamed into the sighted world?'"

"No."

"Is there a political movement of any size that is like the more radical ethnic minority movements in saying that sighted people have to meet us on our own terms. For example, they might say, 'I'm going to live in a house and never turn on the lights or hang up pictures and let sighted people deal with it. Let them come into my world.'"

"No, there is not. Most blind people will try to accommodate." She sounds more angry than sad. "I always turn lights on." Abby is the one blind person I have met who I imagined would take on this issue, at least if her own publicity about herself is to be believed.

"Every once in a while, I'm working on something and Zach comes into the room and says, 'You're working in the dark.' I do know that turning on your outside front porch light at night helps light up the sidewalk and lets your neighbors know that someone is there. There's a certain feeling of human existence going on when they see a light in the kitchen. I will also turn on the lights so that the dog has light. When we were kids, my mother would put the lights on for herself and flip them off if she left the house. Every once in a while we'd have a sighted friend over and she'd forget, and when she was walking out she'd shut off the light and we'd have to say, 'Mom, we've got company.'"

Abby laughs, once again successfully diverting herself from more painful emotions.

"I remember the first time that I put labels on the washing machine at our house when I was still in high school. I was so proud of myself because I had labeled everything in Braille and I could turn the stops and work the machine. My mom came in and said, 'You covered all the switches with black labeling tape and now the rest of us can't use it.'"

We laugh, and Abby continues. "There are actually many things in this world that were easier for us to do twenty years ago than they are now. Just try, for example, to buy a microwave that doesn't have a touch-sensitive panel. Just imagine putting your finger on some completely blank thing. What happened to the good old knob that you turned? None of this is designed for the way blind people work. Try to explain the concept of Windows on a computer to a blind person. It's organizing everything in a visual layout. One of the reasons that this Braille computer that I showed you is so popular is because it is precisely that. It is just set up for a blind person to enter on a Braille keyboard. It requires a word-processing program that is designed from the ground up to be for blind people in the way that we organize things. For example, with a menu, I have to sit and wait for my screen reader to read the entire thing. You see the whole big picture. You can just take the screen and quickly scan on to what you want. We read line by line."

I tell her it seems to me that she and other blind people have to fit into our sighted way of doing things. "I'm trying to understand what your world would be if you were not translating into ours. Does it seem like that to you? As if you're translating it back and forth all the time?"

"Oh yes, absolutely, because you're always trying to think in two different systems."

"It seems like it prevents you from learning what your primary language would be because you're so busy translating into the sighted language. What do you think it would be like if everyone were blind?" I ask.

"Well, you wouldn't have name tags at conventions," Abby quips. We laugh.

"I always feel at a tremendous disadvantage when somebody can walk up to me and say, 'Hi, Abby,' and I can only say, 'Hi, who are you?'"

"Do you think there would be less taboo about touching?"

"I'll never forget one time I got on the bus and someone came up to me and said I remember you. Of course, I was clueless about who she was. She said, "What I really remember about you is the day you got on the bus and you let everyone touch your face. I said, 'Not me, honey.'"

I laugh. "Why did she think it was you?"

"I have no idea, but you'd be amazed at how many people have the notion that I really learn something about a person by touching their face."

"You see that all the time in books and movies about blind people."

"Actually it's a common joke when two blind people meet. We'll sort of poke fun at it and we'll walk up and pretend like we're going to touch their face and ask, 'What's your name?' A face is not how I differentiate, and I don't have enough experience of, say, looking at a crowd of people even to know what different noses are. There are noses that are longer and there are noses that are square. All these different things that have meaning to you have no meaning to me."

"So it would almost be as if I touched somebody's elbow and tried to recognize who they were."

"That's right up there with 'Do you dream in color?' We get that all the time, but it has no meaning. Now what does have meaning are people's voices, the kinds of expressions that they use, the way they walk or move and even the way they breathe.

"You can also do things with your face to show degrees of feeling that I can't do. It's a visually learned kind of skill (Ekman 2012). So for instance when I smile, it tends to be like a really big smile. A lot of expressions may appear on my face, but I am probably not aware of them. I can't call them up consciously. Sometimes, if I tell a story or explain something, the other person may think that I am exaggerating, but I have to convince you that this is damn important to me. My intensity of feeling has to be in my voice. I can't convey it with facial expressions. So I also get labeled a hysterical female very quickly by sighted people."

I ask if she ever used a cane.

"I had a cane before I got my dog. Once I was approaching a very busy intersection and concentrating very hard because I heard noisy traffic all around me. As I was waiting for the light to change to cross, this person came up, grabbed my arm, and proceeded to try to escort me across the street. He happened to grab an arm that was in a great deal of pain.

"I told the guy, 'I don't know what your intentions are when you grab me.' When I finally got to the other side, I got away from him as fast as possible and went on my way. When I arrived at my destination, which happened to be the physical therapy treatment center, I found out that the therapist had seen the whole thing. She was in her car waiting at the light. From her point of view, a nice man came by and helped me across the street. Neither one of our perceptions was totally incorrect, but we're working with different sets of information. I couldn't see a friendly look on his face, which she could see."

"Or how he was dressed," I add. "Or all the ways he could look safe or unsafe to a sighted person."

"Also if you are a blind person out there with a cane, people do walk up and tease you. They pick up the end of your cane and hang onto it. It's amazing how many grown adults will do it. Kids will come up and throw things in my path or come up into my face."

"I can't believe that," I say, quickly shifting to another subject. I am disturbed by what she's told me.

"How do you know if I'm listening or if I have something to say?" I ask. "Or whether to keep talking or stop? All the things that I would code visually in a conversation?"

"Well, you're pretty easy because you're not shy about jumping in when you have something to say, but I'm used to using verbal cues."

At last it is an advantage to have that New Yorker's impatience with the slow unwinding of a thought. In this conversation I have indulged that proclivity for just the reasons we are discussing. How would she know that I want to speak unless I do? To wait would have a dampening effect on the conversation, exactly the opposite of what I am trying to achieve.

"So if you don't get the words, then you don't know what's going on. If I were to sit here quietly, what would happen?"

"I'd think, 'Is she asleep? Is she still here?' I have a really hard time with that. For example, Zach's family is very quiet. When his parents come to visit, I never know whether they have fallen asleep in front of the TV or whether they have left the room, so I get up and walk around and if I run into their knees, I know they are still there.

"The other thing is sighted people who pace so that my ear has to follow them. You guys must get that visually because your eyes follow them. For me, one of the things that I can do to help the person stay focused with me is to face them. And, of course, I have been taught that when I'm interviewing you I don't turn away when I talk to you."

"I've noticed that blind people are trained to do that," I tell Abby.

"If you're not looking at me, chances are that you're going to look at something else. Your attention will wander and you may not listen to me. You know, one of the concepts that my sister and I had a really hard time with when we were little was that if we couldn't see somebody else, then they were not there for us. We assumed that they couldn't see or even hear us either. We had a hard time learning, for example, that we couldn't say something about my aunt who was over in the corner without her hearing us."

I ask if she and her sister face each other when they talk.

"Yes. Still, facing you is not my natural way, but I have been doing it so long that it seems natural by now. Another difference between blind and sighted is the actual degree of body movement. Even though you are not moving much, your eyes are always moving. You're always looking around and kind of putting the whole picture together. If you watch a lot of blind kids, they're walking back and forth. They're moving their heads around a lot. As you grow up, you get taught that this looks wrong to sighted people."

"Oh, so you think that's the equivalent of me scanning with my eyes."

"I do. I have become quite convinced that that's what it is."

"Blind people get told very young that shaking your head around is not acceptable school behavior, so you've got to figure out how to replace its function. I always tell Zach, when we talk about the different ways we argue, that, when I'm talking to you, I am not focused on anything else. The rest of my environment does not exist. I just focus on the words. Also, for example, Zach may spill something that he is pouring, but I almost never do. He misses because he's trying to do too many things at one time.

"All of my roommates in college who were about at my same level of cooking skills had twice as many kitchen disasters as I did, because I wouldn't put something on the stove and walk away to do something else. Generally, I am slower at doing something than you might be. I have to do things one at a time. In some respects, I view people's voices as a more accurate representation of their feelings because they haven't figured out how to fake it. Every blind person that I've brought this up with agrees with me that it is easy to identify someone who has never had sight."

"From the voice?"

"We've all tried to figure out what it is. The only thing we can figure out is maybe there is something about the way that your facial muscles work or something that affects how your voice sounds. We've all had trouble putting our finger on it, yet we've all said the same thing."

"Do you think it's a different intonation?"

"Well, there are muscles around your eyes that are right near your sinuses that do things. It's a bit more nasal."

"For example, some of us will have the radio on and somebody will call a talk show and we can tell if they're blind before they say so.

"There are more discussions recently about body language, about how sighted people will see a certain event versus how we might see it. Because there are so many more blind people that are adults and out in the world these days, I'd say I've heard more discussions of this type in the last three years than I have in all my adult life.

"I think, for instance, if I'm having a bad day and I'm a sighted person and you come up to me, I can very quickly size you up by looking at you—friendly or not friendly. I don't have any of the precursor stuff of what kind of approach you're making, whether you look like somebody that I want to be with or not."

"So you also don't get a choice about when you have privacy or not."

"Right. Gabby and I have talked about this a lot. Are we the only people in the universe who have stood on a street corner and cried? And then, on top of it, we have to refuse your assistance without making you think we have this big chip on our shoulder."

I think about it. I certainly have never done it nor have I ever seen anyone stand on a street corner and cry. Most people would want to be protected from being seen. As a psychologist, I might attribute quite a bit more distress to someone crying in public rather than seeking privacy. But where is the line between private and public if not in the visual cortex? If no one is visible to you, as Abby mentioned, then why should you assume that you are visible to him or her? And why would you define privacy visually? We are certainly living in a world where the concept of privacy is rapidly fading, as people talk on cell phones incessantly in public and post all their thoughts and activities on Facebook and Twitter.

Abby continues. "You'd be surprised at how many complete strangers will just walk up and say, 'Oh, your collar needs straightening' and then grab my collar. Would you want someone to do that to you?"

Actually I dislike it even when people I know do it. It just feels intrusive. This makes me think of something related. I ask Abby if she has a concept of what being stared at is.

"I think so. There's a big presence that you know just isn't going to leave. At college everyone shared a large bathroom. The first time I went to take a shower, I felt like somebody was watching me. I turned around and there was another student watching me to see if I took a shower the same way that she did.

"It also happens a lot when I go out to eat with friends. Most of them are pretty cool about it, but it is a common occurrence for me to get my fork up to my mouth just to discover that there's nothing on it. We call them 'air potatoes.' It feels very unfair because I can't watch you. When we go out, I feel very much that I am the only person who ever spills anything or whoever makes a mess—because I don't ever see you do it."

I am getting the idea that it is burdensome for her to be seen and not see. Maybe she genuinely doesn't know what being stared at is. Of course, she would only know if someone had described it, and clearly, if she does have an idea, it is in that second language that I am coming to recognize. It does not flow from direct experience. Still I decide to try again just to be sure.

"But do you think that you have a concept of what it is to be stared at, or do you think that you learned it? I mean eating in public and also maybe being naked and having other people seeing you in the shower."

"Well, what I pick up is either what isn't happening in the verbal cues or I'll hear you move around occasionally. I'll hear something happening, and I can tell when the movement gets really still if someone is staring."

She is clearly translating, trying to figure out what the sighted person is experiencing. I change my strategy. Although I am interested in her translating, I want to go deeper, to where translation might no longer be required, to her own sensory experience.

"It's like the Bible story of the Garden of Eden." I begin. "Did the apple from the tree of knowledge confer sight or some other kind of knowledge? Does it matter if you can't see that someone is naked? In other words, what if blind people invented the world? Would anyone have to wear clothes except if they were cold?"

"Well I suspect that the answer is yes only because certain parts that are not covered really hurt when you run into something."

We laugh again.

"Clothes would be designed for protection," Abby continues.

"There definitely would be more texture in clothing. I've noticed that sometimes Zach will say something like, 'There are two tops in your closet and they're exactly alike.' I'll say, 'They're not alike at all. They're completely different kinds of material."

Clothing would cover parts of bodies differently. What would the world be like if everyone went blind? I can tell you that stairs would be very different if blind people ran the world."

"Stairs? How?"

"Think about all the flights of stairs architecturally designed because they're pretty. Think about how you walk up and down those stairs. They're not even. They're not even three steps and then a flat space and then three more steps and then a flat space. And you're going downhill all the time. It's an awful experience if you can't see what you're doing."

I remind her that she said similar things about how she experiences a table.

"Actually I had an experience when I was living in my first apartment in Ohio up on the seventh floor. The fire alarm went off one night. It was the middle of January, so it was twenty below. It was ten thirty at night. We had to go down the outdoor fire escape on metal steps with spaces in between them. Of course, they were all icy and I had no shoes on. I had just jumped out of the shower. My hair was full of shampoo. I had a dog at the time, and my dog and I were walking as quickly as I could safely go down those stairs. It wasn't really slow, but every time I got down one flight, we had to turn, find the next edge and continue on the next flight again. Well, there were so many people piling up behind me that they did not have the patience for just that little quick step I was doing at the top of the landing. By the time I was down to about the fourth floor, I had to be rescued by the fire department or I would have been trampled to death. People were running right over me."

As I listen carefully to her reasonable perspective on this event, I also imagine the panic of the sighted participants trying desperately to flee the burning building as quickly as possible. Both viewpoints make total sense from inside their own experience. This experience is congealed around life-times of sight or nonsight and is either sense or non-sense to the participants.

Lacking vision is not the same as lacking other senses. Abby reflects on the differences between being blind and being deaf. "If I can't hear you, then I don't have your words or your concepts, so I can't enter your world as easily as a blind person who has all the language. I have a friend who taught at Gallaudette University for a while.

I said, 'Tell me how you carry on a conversation at lunch and eat tacos or spaghetti?'"

Again, we laugh together, making light of a subject we both know is serious.

"Kids' questions are the best," Abby tells me. "They will come up and say, 'If you can't see, how do you go to the bathroom?'" More laughter.

"You've got to give them credit for having the courage to spit it out."

"Or they do it because they think I am also in the same child category. I swear when I'm sixty years old there will still be people out there calling me 'that sweet little blind girl.' Sighted people do tend to treat blind people as if they were children, get in their space and touch them even.

"Here is another dynamic that is very difficult for a blind person. We're at a party. There's a crowd of people. Think about what you do when you min-gle. You can make eye contact with somebody that you see across the room. Let's say we're walking around just kind of listening and there's somebody I know. Now how do I let them know that I've just spotted them? Do I break into their conversation and say 'Hi'? You can get their visual attention very quickly and easily move around the room and talk with a lot of people. Also it takes really being extroverted to be able to approach people you cannot see."

Abby turns to another topic that is clearly important to her.

"Everybody loves you if you are a blind person and you're successful. When you mention something about a blind person, the first thing people will do is tell you about this one blind person who did something extraordinary. He built a house. He swam the English Channel. He sailed around the world."

As Abby talks, I think about the developing genre of books about the extraordinary accomplishments of a particular blind person. I've read most of these books by now. Does the story of a blind person have to be extraordinary and inspirational to come to the attention of a sentimental reading public? I think there is a lot of truth to the idea.

"I think that we have the right to succeed or be ordinary or even lazy just as much as anyone else does. Equality isn't being able to have the top job in the world filled by a blind person. Yet, if you turn on the news, you hear a story about a blind person climbing Mt. Whitney in the name of blind people to show that we're capable of something.

"It comes up a lot in relationships, in marriage. For example, when Zach and I go out for a walk, he wants to describe what we're passing. Sometimes it's very enjoyable to know something about what you're passing, but other times I don't care, and especially because it can never go in the other direction. I'm very seldom in the position of explaining the environment to him. I can get overwhelmed very quickly and then I'll get to the point where I'll say, "Stop. I don't want you to explain. I just want to carry on a conversation."

She is in her own world and not wanting to be compelled to join that of the sighted person by her side, in this case her husband, Zach. "Join me in my world," she cries. Come to me. Don't make me always come to you." Here is a serious glimpse of how blind people learn to pass, to speak a second language, in this poignant cry to let up the incessant pressure.

Abby goes on. "It becomes very difficult to define what I'm contributing to sighted people because I need them so much. There are certain tasks that I have to do in life that just, flat out, I must have a sighted person to help. There are gonna be times when there's no way that I can understand why something happened because there's something about the situation that's visual that I don't know. Somebody has to tell me. Or I have to go someplace and have to have somebody drive me. Does it ever go the other way? What kind of need do I fill in them? Before Zach and I got married, for instance, we had a very long discussion about making sure why he was marrying me. It wasn't a matter of feeling sorry for me and marrying me to take care of me, because it was going to be all wrong if he did. Sometimes, if I've had a day where everybody has been coming up and patting me on the head and pushing me around, then I have to define what safety is at home. After a day like that, I come up against something that is tough to do. You come up and want to help me and you're my husband. I'm going to bite your head off. I'm feeling that I have been pushed around all day, so I am going to do this myself if it takes until midnight. But if I had a day in which I had to figure out something by myself and sort things out that were complicated, then my definition of safety is that I don't have to prove anything at home. So consequently my husband often doesn't know what the situation is.

"We often have miscues over when to help me and when not to help because he's the one that I've got enough safety with to be real. You can be sort of polite with somebody who's just passing by, but not with somebody you're with all the time. So I eventually had to explain to him why it looked to him like I can be so gracious with everybody else and I'm less forgiving with him. I can use him to kind of balance the input I've had for the rest of the day."

"But I suppose you had to develop a kind of way of saying that to each other."

"It's such a big American myth also that we have to do everything for ourselves anyway."

"And having to prove that you're capable all the time."

"The process of trying to be accepted can be very lonely. There are certain ways in which, as a blind person, you are always going to be a little bit of an outsider. You have certain attachments, but there are always certain things that are going to make it a different experience. That part makes me think of the ways that it would be easier to have your partner be another blind person rather than a sighted person. But, by the same token, if Zach were blind, we certainly would not have hopped in the car and driven up to Canada or hiked the Sierras. I hope you know," she says, laughing, "I wouldn't have gotten on the road for a second."

I am getting the rhythm of serious comment followed by a joke that is Abby's way of revealing herself to me.

"In many ways it's easier to be a blind woman and to have a sighted husband than it is to be a blind man and have a sighted wife. Harder for a man to feel like a man."

This is precisely what Samantha and Luke had also said to me.

"Very often it will be the sighted wife who has the job and the blind man can't find one. And there is the problem with who does the domestic chores. When Zach and I moved from our last place, the owner called to ask Zach to clean the oven a little better. I was the one who had cleaned it, but she assumed that I couldn't. I said to her, 'Look, I'm perfectly willing to accept that the oven wasn't up to your standards and even that you want to take something off the deposit, but don't just assume that Zach did it.'

"It is easier for me to do the women's work than it is for a man who is blind to play this role. Yet I can't do everything that a sighted woman would do. It might become very important to me and be no big deal to you. It can become a very precious thing if you're fighting for it all the time. So you can develop a very different way of looking at just a little ordinary thing. Because there are so many times when you just have to let go. So it's a balancing act. And then there are just some times when being blind is a royal nuisance, like if you have one of those days where people come up and spit at you."

"Spit at you? I can't believe it!" I can't easily take this in. "Why would they spit at you?"

"I don't know. It's bullying, I guess, just to see if they get a reaction. So I don't give them one. I just keep going. What I will allow myself to do is to set a time limit when I get home. I'll say to myself, 'You can go bury your head in the pillow and cry for half an hour.' I allow myself a certain amount of time to say that this happened and my reaction to it was normal, that I don't deserve to have something like that done to me. I just try to keep it in perspective and to keep myself from getting too dragged down by it.

"My sister is much quicker to holler at somebody than I am. She always has been, but most of the time I try to ignore them. With a dog, I feel a little more entitled to claim my space on the sidewalk.

"You know, one of the funniest things that ever happened to me was in crossing a really busy intersection." Here comes the joking part again. It's an effective defense and one with which I am personally familiar. It highlights the absurdity of it all, while releasing some of the pain, at least temporarily.

Abby goes on with her story. "When you step off the curb, you cross to one of these traffic islands. It's real skinny front to back but long left to right.

OK? So I came up on this island and there's the walk light pole on the island. I know this island so well. I've done it so many times that I step up on the island and I hear the pole on my right. So my right hand automatically goes out because I know that it's there. And my thumb is in a position to push the button to change the light. One day while I was doing this, I pushed on another person instead of the button. I could not have aimed better. My thumb right on the nipple. Of course I immediately jumped. And said, 'Oh, I'm sorry.' I was also startled because, quite frankly, I had never felt a breast that big in my life. It was six months before I punched that walk light again. I was just blown away because I had no concept that people got that big."

It's a good story, and I laugh appreciatively before asking the question I've been asking every blind person I meet.

"If you could have sight for twenty-four hours?"

She responds readily; it's clear she has given thought to this issue. Who wouldn't?

"I wouldn't want it for only twenty-four hours. Then I would just have to miss it again. I'd like to see Zach's face when he looks at me. The look he gives me. My dog. Everyone says he is beautiful. I'd want to go to Paris. See how cities look different. Walk down the sidewalk at my own pace anywhere I wanted to. Cross the street at any angle I felt like. And I'd be able to go off myself to remote places. Camp in the mountains, for example. And if you want to cast certain looks. I mean there are people in the street that I'd love to give them a look that says 'drop dead.' I can't give you a quick look that says 'Keep your distance.' Faces are very important to you, but not to us. A face is not how I differentiate.

"There are certain ways in which I am always going to be an outsider. I had a roommate once who tried to teach me how to make faces—how to raise an eyebrow. You don't get clues from my facial expression, so I have to explain what I am feeling."

Abby's comments and my own observations strongly contradict Eckman's (1993) idea that all people across the globe exhibit the same facial expressions for the same emotions. While he reports having found this even in the blind, I've noticed that often an emotion is not signaled or expressed with any facial expression at all. When used, facial expressions are often extreme exaggerations of those of the sighted.

I have learned so much from my time with Abby. As is apparent, she is intelligent, passionate, and has a lively sense of humor that is always at the ready. I was touched by her honesty and her courage not only in navigating a sighted world but in telling the best truth that she could about her experiences. Her comments were invaluable for me in putting some of the pieces of this story together. I was beginning to be able to perceive the first language of the congenitally blind, touch, and the fragmentation that it entailed. Ironically, understanding this fragmentation was helping me to perceive the whole picture.

9

Double Blind

GABRIELLE

We scarcely know how much of our pleasure and interest in life comes to us through our eyes until we have to do without them; and part of that pleasure is that the eyes can choose where to look. But the ears can't choose where to listen.

—URSULA K. LE GUIN

I TRIED TO MEET ABIGAIL and her twin sister, Gabrielle, together, but I finally gave up just on the cusp of becoming annoying to them. How many times could I ask? They jealously guard their shared time and do not want to permit intrusion. Knowing how close they are as twins, both blinded at birth, I cannot say that I blame them. Not only would they have lost their precious time together, our conversation would have been complicated and challenging. There would be so much to explain, so many words required, and all these words in my language rather than in theirs. Even though they resist a joint meeting, Gabby is as willing as Abby was to meet with me on her own.

Gabby lives in a part of Oakland with which I am familiar, and one day, a few weeks after the afternoon I spent with her twin, I find myself standing at her front door. She lives in an old California-style bungalow in a pleasant, working-class neighborhood of Oakland. I walk up the three stairs to the wooden front porch and knock on the large old-fashioned oak door. When Gabby opens the door, I am startled by the obvious physical differences between her and Abby. Gabby is much shorter, with different hair color and features, and seems much quieter in demeanor and voice. She does not reach out to me in any way, physical or psychological. She is warm enough, but reserved.

Both twins have told me that they are "identical," but they apparently mean something different by this term from what the sighted mean, and perhaps even the geneticists. I am not sure whether or not they share one set of chromosomes, but my eyes suggest otherwise. Of course, they would have had to be told that they are identical. Perhaps their mother wanted to strengthen their bond. On the other hand, recent genetic data has demonstrated that many pairs of twins who can see believe that they are identical when the DNA says otherwise (Wright 1997).

Gabby has different facial features, except for the identical artificial eyes surgically implanted when they were both young children. It is the first time I have encountered this surgical alternative, which was a medical necessity for them. Gabby is more somber in appearance and I would not have guessed that Abby is her twin. Certainly experience, and not just biology, contributes to appearance, the manner in which one carries oneself, the facial expressions and gestures. But could it account for Gabby being shorter, which she is by an inch or two? I am seeing for myself how much experience molds appearance, how much nature must be nurtured, how intertwined the two are. I will not find out the genetic answer, as they both insist they are identical twins.

When I mention to Gabby that she does not look exactly like Abby, she smiles and says nothing. After all, what can she say? She could tell me what other sighted people say about that—or not. She chooses the latter.

It is immediately apparent that Gabby is more of an introvert and less of a performer than her sister. She is quieter in every way, including the physical. It does not take a psychologist to see that, but it does take a pair of eyes. Gabby is cordial and less effusive than her twin, but eager to make me feel comfortable and to talk about her life. She invites me across the worn threshold of her house without a hug or a handshake. We settle down in a living room clearly decorated by and for sighted people. There are pictures in groups on the walls and matching colors of furniture.

Like Abby, Gabby is married to a sighted man; they have been together for more than ten years. The sisters live in different cities as a result of their husbands' jobs. This separation means they cannot be as close as they were growing up, and it's one reason they treasure their time together so much. I'm impressed that Abby and Gabby both have stable and satisfying marriages. It's a testament to the excellent training that their mother provided. She instilled in them the self-confidence to do anything to which they put their minds, even though it might be more difficult without sight. She really did her job. They both have successful careers and marriages that work for them.

In recent months, Gabby and Abby have both traded in their white canes, or "the stick," as they call it, for guide dogs they are training together. During those sessions the two sighted husbands sometimes watch soccer on television or go to a nearby park to participate in a local soccer match. The men share that common interest. While they also share the experience of being married to blind sisters, they choose not to discuss that experience. To them, it is just life and not unique enough to require words. This is the kind of men they both are.

I ask Gabby several of the questions I have developed from my previous meetings with blind people and especially some of the same questions I asked Abby.

"How did being a twin help or interfere in your childhood?"

"Well, it helped more than I can tell you. I don't know what my life would have been like otherwise. We totally understood each other and even had one of those secret languages. When a day was difficult for me or for her, we knew exactly who would understand. The same when one of us had a special success, like a good performance or a new skill.

"In adolescence, we both realized that the time was coming for each of us to go separately into the outside world. We didn't want to be the kind of twins who don't have other relationships or dress identically all through their lives. There is a pair of them in San Francisco. They dress identically and wander around downtown every day. Everyone in the city knows about them. That is too much for me. Abby and I are fierce about developing our own identities."

Identical is really a misnomer for any two people, I suddenly realize. Identical DNA may be a more accurate expression. However, the world has known about twins much longer than anyone has known about the existence of DNA, so the lack of descriptive accuracy is understandable in a way. They are far from mirror images of each other, but neither of them would know much about what a mirror is. They both speak the language of the mirror well enough to seem fluent, but they are not. They are translating.

Gabby has a small practice focused on reading auras and energy. Even in the New Age of the San Francisco Bay area, it is extremely unusual for a person who doesn't have "first sight" to be a master of "second sight." Yet I try to reserve judgment as much as I can until I can discern if this ability is genuine or a compensation for her missing vision. We discuss the feelings of different energies, whether animate or inanimate. Gabby maintains that both give off a kind of energy that she experiences and by which she is strongly affected. We delve into this topic with consideration of the artwork that is around us. I have talked about visual representations with all the blind men and women I've met, and I am about to hear a slightly new angle.

"Why would you put paintings on the wall if it weren't for sighted people?"

I suppose it's partly for sighted people, and of course in some of the work I do I'm seeing clients. I want to create a certain atmosphere. We have a piece of artwork in the hall now that depicts snow and winter. I don't get what's in the picture at all. It has an odd feel to it. It has an interesting texture, but, when I first moved in, my husband had it above the bed in the bedroom. After about a week, I said, 'You have to move this thing. I can't stand sleeping under it.' He moved it into the hall and hung something else in the bedroom."

"What replaced it?" I ask, but interestingly she does not remember and does not offer to let me see for myself. Instead we continue our conversation.

"I know it affects me. It affects my living environment. I can't pinpoint exactly how, but it does. The last thing I hung in my office was a tapestry on the closet door. As soon as I brought it in here and held it up to the closet door, I had the feeling that it warms up the room."

I understand from these comments that somehow warm feeling is preferable to cold in Gabby's lexicon.

"Everything in the office is art that I've brought into our home." Gabby tells me. "This one is the streets of Paris and this long one is parchment paper. They're not framed in glass. I love the frames and the grain in the wood. There are a couple of things out in the hallway, like my father's license plate from the old truck he drove when we were kids. There is also a little tapestry that has a nice velvety texture and I love to go and feel that. I have other things, like the altar on red velvet that's behind you, and I'll feel that. I like the feeling of having life in the room. I would put more live things around, but my husband just seems to be terribly allergic to them."

"I would think that you would decorate the room, but why pictures on the wall? Why not flowers or oranges and bananas?"

"For one, they're harder to hang on the wall. I don't want it to be so much 'Come into the world of the blind person.' I want it to be a world that can accommodate a lot of different people. I do hesitate to hang things. If you go in the bathroom, you'll see a map of Middle Earth a friend did for me. It's kind of embroidered; when I first moved in, I had a lot of stuff like that. My husband said, 'Well, we can hang your stuff, but it's sort of home-spun. It doesn't have the same status as art. It's too bad because it takes as much knowledge of art and as much creativity.'"

There has been much written on craft as women's work that has been devalued over the centuries by that same masculine gaze that is in charge of defining feminine beauty (Chicago and Lucie-Smith 1999; Deepwell 2013; Freeland 2001; Hein 2010, 2011; Light and Smith 2004; Millett-Gallant 2010). There has been much less written about tactile beauty and art, although it has been considered by some feminist critics in recent years (Scheman 1993; Ziarek 2012a, b). I myself am a fan of so-called outsider art, both painting and craftwork. How would I explain the difference between officially sanctioned and outsider art to a blind person? I do not try.

"What about outside this room, something less abstract like a sunset?"

"I don't have a clue about a sunset. I get nothing, although I know that a sunset means the sun disappears. And the sun rises. I don't even understand how that concept translates visually. How can the sun suddenly appear or disappear? The sun is always there; it's moving and suddenly it just disappears. People talk about the sun disappearing over the horizon. As many times as people have tried to explain it to me, I don't have anywhere in my understanding to put that concept."

"It's like the sky. How would you have a concept of the sky?"

"It's just space out there. Clouds are also a funny concept. Now fog I understand because I can feel it."

"What if I ask you something like what your mother's face looks like?"

"I can imagine what it must be. I can imagine that she would look a little careworn. I think of her face as sort of fragile and sort of bony, but I don't think of it in terms of what is her nose like or her chin or her mouth or her forehead. I know, for instance, that the way that she often told my sister and me apart when we were little was the difference in foreheads. I think it was me that I had the higher forehead." So she knows that they are not identical, albeit in terms learned from her mother.

"She must smile some, and people must see softness, but do they see the tigress that's going to get through anything?"

I imagine that if I asked sighted people about their mothers' faces, they would also respond in terms of feelings, as Gabby has. I think of my own mother's face as a small test of this issue; the image, imbued with feelings, appears for me long before the words. I suspect that this is typical of the sighted. There is so much emotion embedded in the image of one's mother.

"Last night we had a friend over, and my husband pulled out some pictures that his mother had of him when he was younger, high school or early college age. She passed away, so now he has them, and I found myself asking what he looked like. They said 'Like himself.' 'Well,' I said, 'you guys can do better than that.' I kept pressing them. 'Did he look like a happy kid? Did he have more of a glow? Did he look miserable?' I never did get an answer." She can never answer these questions for herself, so it will remain a mystery.

"I remember once in junior high or high school hearing some TV thing where they talked about how, with twins, one tends to be the dominant and one tends to be the shadow. I don't know if it's true, but there was something about the way that it was said that scared me."

"Which one were you afraid of being?" I ask.

"I don't know because at that moment I tended to be the dominant one and she was the shadow."

I am surprised that she was the dominant one. Things change, I suppose. I comment, "You both are pretty strong personalities. Nobody's shadow either one of you."

Gabby nods and goes on.

"But I think we had to get away from each other to do that. Even now, as my husband puts it, 'the two of you getting together is quite a force, and the rest of us kind of run away.' As long as I was with her I had to get away. I had to find out who I was as a whole person. We weren't a whole person, so we had to do a little separating to find out. I don't think that she necessarily cared to find out. She was the serious student. She was the hard worker. She was much happier being a loner."

I turn the conversation to the topic of race.

"Abby and I come in contact with different racial groups because of where we live," Gabby points out. "Graton is a lot whiter than Oakland. I lived near Graton for a few years. I was a technician at a local radio station there. We were always getting it from the FDC for not having enough minorities. They couldn't give us any flack about the disabled portion. That was me. There was another guy who was in a wheelchair, but we were both white. What can you do? Go hire somebody who's not qualified?"

I don't answer. I am not looking for a debate on affirmative action at this moment. I tend to avoid these sorts of issues anyway, putting my energy into activities that are more likely to have a payoff than convincing someone to change their position on this issue.

"It kind of struck me," Gabby says. "It was noticeable to me when I moved here that there are a lot of minorities."

"How did you notice it?"

"Language. I was thinking a lot in the last couple of days that most of my cues are verbal—an accent in most cases. Here in Oakland, particularly in this area, there are a lot of Chinese. We're very close to Chinatown. So I'm always going into stores that are owned by Chinese, Vietnamese, or other people who cannot speak English. How do I get served?" she asks rhetorically.

"If I am confronted with a group and having difficulty getting a need met or getting something to happen, my prejudices come up fast. I wish they weren't there, but they are."

She laughs uneasily. "I want to say, 'Don't humiliate me in the process of communicating. It hurts and it makes me very angry.' I notice myself feeling things like 'You're living in this country; learn to say a few words.' I don't like to think of myself that way but there it is."

"So somebody is humiliating you and you think of a way to humiliate them back, to even the score."

"Also it makes me feel like there's nothing I can do. How do I live here? It happens to me all the time. I went into a store to buy tea the other day, but nobody could talk to me. I couldn't do the transaction. I left. I came home and when my husband was running errands he went and got it. How I hate that. I just sat here and cried. I really don't want to be limited or defined as 'Blindy.' That would be like having a black man wear an armband. It would say, 'Look, a black man is coming.'"

I want to say that his black skin, which Gabby has never seen, already serves as a loud announcement in American society. And I wonder if she knows about the yellow armbands that were used to identify Jews in Nazi Germany. I do not want to interrupt her, however, with my associations with armbands.

"My husband and I did a lot of traveling in the South. It was almost impossible for me to tell the different races apart because they all talk with the same accent there. I couldn't tell if someone was black or white, as I can in Oakland. It made me think about things a little bit differently. It made me think about people who are different and about what my own responses are to people I don't understand. As a result, I try more to approach people from other cultures. Doing that has made me feel a little easier with them. I don't have to buy into my own feelings of being intimidated."

Discussing skin color leads her to colors in other places, especially on the fabrics that we use to cover human skin. I follow along.

"I've always been very color conscious. I get the biggest kick out of coordinating clothes. I always remember what color my clothes are. I can see colors in auras also. I would look at you and right away I would get a hit of yellow. I don't really know where that comes from."

"What does it mean to you?" I ask, trying not to sound too yellow.

"It means that you are very analytical, and that your emotional base is not so up in your face at the moment."

"So you would call that yellow? That's the name that you have for it. Well, let me ask you if you get any other sense of me this quickly from my voice or my aura. You say you can tell people's race and different things about them from the way they sound."

"My image of you would be the Caucasian group. Your energy field is larger, and like it goes narrower up here," she gestures toward her head, "expanding out, so I get a sense of more earthiness about you. I would pinpoint you in terms of ethnicity as either Eastern Europe or Russian, a heartier group of people."

This educated guess takes me back instantly to Jesse's idea that I must wear glasses and look intelligent. I don't want to dismiss Gabby's ideas either, but I imagine that my last name suggests this ethnicity to her. However, I came by this Czech surname through marriage, indeed to a heartier person than my own more fearful ancestors.

"To return to colors for a minute," Gabby says, "I find that when I get dressed I pick a color that will help me feel like I want to that day. I need to wear a blue or red to be a little bit bolder and not so afraid of the world."

"Do you ask a sighted person what colors your clothes are?"

"Yeah, do I look good in this color? Does this color work with that color? What image am I creating with a certain color, and do they clash or go together? I usually start out with a kind of feel of my own. They look kind of cool together. I usually get it confirmed," Gabby adds proudly.

"Every once in a while I'll be wrong, but most of the time I'm pretty right on. I can also sense what jewelry will go with certain things."

Again, color is so important that she tries to crack the code, as do so many of the other blind people I have already met. As I think back on the others, I realize that it is the women who emphasize dress and color. By now I am not surprised at this effort to conform to sighted gender expectations. I am still saddened by it. I am also more and more aware of how strong the relationship between most sighted females and their mirrors is. These blind women try desperately to participate in this quintessentially female relationship rather than rejecting it. The other primary relationship, the one with the scale, is easier to transpose to other senses.

I move to a related topic.

"I have found it very interesting to ask people who are blind to whom they are sexually attracted and how they know. I've had people tell me that they knew if they were gay or straight when they were five years old and had their first crushes at that age."

"I didn't know anything about the concept of being gay or straight," she answers a little too quickly.

"I don't remember. I mean I do remember that when I was eight or nine, I had a little boyfriend and, by the time I was ten, I was getting pretty interested in boys."

"Some people have told me that, even in elementary school, they had a crush on a teacher, but I always thought people have crushes on their teacher because they see their teacher," I push on.

Gabby shakes her head.

"They hear them. I had this Australian flame when I was in Australia. I was going through some tapes the other day and I found a tape that he sent me. I heard one word of this man's voice and I was gone. Oh, yeah. Voices will do it to me."

Research with mirror neurons that are so involved in human empathy has recently revealed that these mirrors in the brain become tuned to sound and hearing in the blind (Ricciardi et al. 2009), so this preference is understandable. We have yet to learn about the neuroscience of sexual attraction in the sighted or the blind. But, with the field developing so rapidly, I'm sure this knowledge is not far away. Perhaps my questions about attraction will one day seem old-fashioned.

Gabby has warmed to the topic of sexual attraction.

"With my husband he had a sort of seductive way of using his voice that definitely got my attention. I bet if you closed your eyes and somebody who you were going to be attracted to came and stood next to you, you would feel the chemistry." She is as confident about her own primary sensory experience as I am that this would not happen to me. I can't imagine any sort of attraction without being able to look into that person's eyes.

"I have a cross-country skiing partner," Gabby tells me, "who is very close to the ideal of 'tall, dark, and handsome.' He's kind of tall, and his body is in shape. You can feel the muscles in his legs and arms, which are also a little rough. I have never gone out with a guy like that. My husband isn't like that at all, and sometimes I'll get on him a little bit about exercise and why he doesn't take care of his body."

I resist asking her how she came to feel her skiing partner's legs. After all, she is still recovering from my question about gay or straight attractions. Instead I ask the perhaps more obvious question.

"Where did you get the idea about 'tall, dark and handsome'?"

"I don't know. That is the sort of thing that everybody says. From the standpoint of touch, I really like the feel of a body that's well groomed and muscular. I have some very intimate women friends, but I definitely have a sexual leaning toward men and not women. Some blind people I've known really got into a lot of sexual experimentation with women and men. They would just say, 'I don't see what they look like, so why should I care?' I have never been that way.

"Sometimes when I was single I wondered, 'Do I have a choice when I date?' I had the image in high school that all the popular guys and all the popular girls must be good-looking. I must be ugly because I'm not in the 'in crowd.' So I've had this idea I could never date the good-looking guys.

"As I got older, I started going a little bit more for other qualities. I've always been a little bit conscious of my own image and whether I am attractive or not. Do they see me or just another blind person? Do they see my good qualities? 'She has a nice smile or she dresses well.' I don't think about myself as good-looking."

"What do you think? How do you see yourself?"

"Rationally I can say that I dress pretty well and when I'm not working at home I can put on makeup pretty well."

"You use makeup?"

"Mostly lipstick, but when I'm working at home I get very lazy."

An interesting definition of lazy, I think: a blind woman not putting on makeup. Lazy is not what I would call it.

She senses my question.

"Why do I do this? I don't even know if it has an effect. I don't know if it helps my image or not, but every other woman I know does it."

"I was thinking, if I were blind, why would I paint my lips rather than my elbow? Do you know what I mean?"

"It's a way to be attractive to people who are sighted. It makes me feel like I'm marking a special occasion. Going out on the town, I get dressed up. I put makeup on to make it a special occasion."

"It's like putting on high heels."

"That I don't do!" We laugh together.

Just as some people believe in a higher power that is invisible, so must these sisters believe in the sighted world. It takes a certain faith. They are haunted by the specter of sight, by the concepts of color and of gender, among many other ghosts.

I ask the next question.

"What would you do if you had sight for twenty-four hours?"

"I'd love to be like a sighted person with no rules, just stroll or run, stop to window-shop and browse. What would it look like to see a mountain range? I don't lose any sleep over that. I heard the expression last night *the come-hither look*, but I don't know how to translate it into a facial expression.

Almost all the blind people I have met had muted facial expressions. I do remember Abby telling me that she had to exaggerate her facial expressions to be taken seriously, but she never did demonstrate for me. I hope that was because I took her seriously without the slightest push in that direction.

The sighted world has its own elaborate set of rules about what to see and what complex and multiple meanings any visual experience presents, as we are beginning to understand from spending time with these blind individuals. Part of their informal education is being taught how to see gender and race as well as what these mean in various contexts. I discuss these findings in more formal educational settings in the next chapter.

While exposing these rules may be part of my purpose in this book, it is of little consequence to these twins. They are pleased to follow along as best they can, translating into their native tongue. Fortunately for them, they have each other for assistance and company.

10

Blind Citizenship Classes

THE MIRROR DOES NOT REFLECT

Vision is the art of seeing things invisible.

—JONATHAN SWIFT

I HAD ONE MORE STOP ON my journey through blind territory before feeling confident of my observations and conclusions, and that involved visiting a formal institution of learning. Back to school. There is a school for blind children and adolescents not far from the university where I teach in San Jose. I was able to arrange to visit several times along with some of my own students, the ones engaged in this project with me. We set out one morning to spend our first of several days there, a caravan of cars winding down California Highway 101, adding our bulk to the already congested freeway. This is still the California way, perhaps the American way, attachment to the automobile. Traveling from San Jose to Fremont, there are not yet any alternatives.

We were privileged to be able to attend several classes. None was strictly academic, as we might be able to convince ourselves that public schools for the sighted are. In fact, they were all more about socialization than anything else, much like the invisible aspects of "normal" schooling. Here they must be translated carefully and as accurately as possible from the visual to the verbal. Most of us who are sighted learned gender just as we were learning arithmetic, learned racialization as an integral part of history and geography, and had them reinforced during recess and physical education classes.

In my own case, sixth grade was a time I remember vividly, although I had had hundreds and hundreds of subtler lessons along the way. The subtler and more embedded learning is more difficult to resist as it may easily bypass awareness. However, this time it could not have been more deliberate. The girls and the boys were separated to learn about menstruation and the biology of sexuality away from each other's embarrassment-inducing eyes. This was reinforced with dancing lessons and the announcement that we would have a graduation prom and that each boy should ask a girl for a date to this event. We all followed these instructions dutifully. This was still the 1950s after all.

I see this time now as my last few moments of freedom. I was still a "tomboy" and still the class cutup, but the second most popular boy in the class asked me to the dance. It was quite a conquest, as there were many girls prettier than I was. I was not blind. Not a moment of it was fun for either of us, so tense and awkward we were, but we passed this gender test with flying colors.

More covertly, these were the last moments that I would be admired for my intelligence or wit. These now moved irrevocably into the male territory. As a female, I was only to admire them. But I did not, although I eventually learned to fake it in certain circumstance where gender was most salient, such as dating and dancing.

Among these blind students, I was actually delighted to discover more than one of the kind of cutup that I was at their age. After all, why shouldn't learning be fun and why shouldn't learning be cut up? I enjoyed their antics and their liveliness. I knew that the girls especially would outgrow both if the teachers had their way. They would learn instead to giggle appreciatively as the boys joked and played.

These blind students had to be instructed more verbally than I did. I had, if anything, too much experience in understanding what a "dirty look," a raised eyebrow, or a frown meant. They instead depended on the words of the teachers as they could not readily learn by example. They could not watch adults or other adolescents and children for gendered reactions. In the classroom they fidgeted in their seats constantly and moved their heads in every possible direction, not guided by the sight of the instructor or the other children. They appeared restless and in constant motion, but I had already been warned by both Gabby and Abby that the sighted can move their eyes around and the substitute for this ability might be this more apparent physical motion.

Nothing is taught to blind students more carefully than gender-related behaviors and signs. They must be mastered consciously and by intent, not in the same manner that we sighted individuals are taught them, allowing some room for the illusion that they are natural. For the blind, they are based in practice and mimicry, in repeated rehearsal unseen by themselves. The girls are taught to keep their legs together, to walk delicately, to stand straight, and to smile a lot. The boys are taught to be rougher, to take up as much space as they can, and to judge their own worth by the women they attract. With no one to imitate, these lessons are not multisensory or embedded in their bodies unconsciously; they do not result in imitating early caretakers, but come much as my classmates and I learned world history, by memorization. In one classroom I actually listened to a lecture, or more accurately a riff, on the size and placement of belt buckles according to gender. Everyone in the room understood who was to have the bigger ones.

In his book, *Touch the Top of the World,* Erik Weihenmayer (2002) discusses his own dating experiences. Like most of the writing by or about blind men, this book underlines the extraordinary accomplishments possible without vision. There is very little, if anything, written by or about blind women since Helen Keller. I think of this genre as "the blind man as hero," and here are some of the musings of one of these heroes.

In the early winter I sat on a bar stool at the 40th Street Grill drinking a beer with Rob, another teacher at the Phoenix Country Day School, when he said, "You know who you should go after? Ellen Reeve. She's got the most beautiful blue eyes and a very athletic body. Did you know she coaches the boys' soccer team?"

I had set up the conversation brilliantly by asking Rob who the good-looking teachers were, not letting on that I was really most interested in Ellen. Little did I know that Ellen would be at the top of his list.

Rob had gone through the teachers, first highlighting the ones who wore miniskirts barely covering their thighs, next the Ivory girls with wholesome good looks, and finally the older babes who still showed traces of their former beauty. I told him the ones who I thought had hot voices: some with a rough sexy purr, others high pitched and chirpy, and still others rumbling and spit-firing their words quickly and articulately; and Rob would confirm or dispute. Some think that blind people do not care about looks, that we are above assessing one's desirability through surface beauty, but if that's the case, I proudly break the stereotype. I am as much a pig as any sighted guy. In fact, I take offense at those who would assume that just because I am blind I am supposed to be asexual. Blindness has little to do with the virtue or villainy of one's character. I can be just as shallow, but my shallowness comes from the voluptuous hum of a sexy voice or the electrifying grasp of a smooth supple hand.

It is embarrassing the desperate lengths I have gone to learn what a woman looks like while trying to keep alive her angelic impression of me. Once I met a woman on the train back to Boston. We had talked and laughed together the whole way home. She had a clear pleasant voice, but although the connection between a sexy voice and a shapely body is often accurate, it is still a big risk to proceed by the sound of a voice alone. At the end of the ride I had gotten the courage to ask her out. When at last I met her for our date, I shook her hand and was a little worried. She had not passed the hand test: short, fat, stubby fingers nine times out of ten means a short, fat, stubby body; and, now standing, I was aware of her voice projecting from a long way down. I arranged for us to go have pizza at Geo's Pizza in Harvard Square where my friend conveniently worked behind the counter. I shook his hand as I introduced her and knew, instantly, my growing alarm was well justified. He had shaken my hand with his fingers curled and cupped together, forcing my hand to curl and cup in return. He had given me the ugly shake and there was nothing for me to do but to finish out the date.

(142–43)

I have been told many versions of this story. I have now witnessed blind girls and boys being trained to this sighted standard in their schools. And finally I have seen it for myself, the concern of blind men not just for a sighted partner, but for one considered attractive by sighted standards. What does the appearance of a woman mean to a blind man? Almost exactly what it means to many well-socialized men. I think we know by now what that is. It means something about his own masculinity. It means that he has been trained in gender, and that gender is an invention of the culture that defines it and not "natural," not a biological necessity. Better said, gender is a complex, evolving combination of nature and nurture constantly being altered by multiple feedback loops between experience and various aspects of the human brain (Kaschak 2010). Studies have shown that the behavior of boys and girls is often more traditionally gendered when there are males present (Kaschak and Sharratt 1985, 1988). Just as it is possible to train dogs, horses, and other species to become show animals, to move and stand and prance in certain ways, so it is with humans, only more so, as humans produce so many more complex behaviors in addition to responding to context sensitively.

Between classes, the students swarm outdoors where they tumble and crash into each other in a rowdy enactment of adolescent exuberance. Here and there some older teenagers have already paired off and are heading for their favorite bench or spot of grass. Their sense of play and their hormones seem to be working just fine. Yet they had to be broken by the teachers like potential, but still wild, racehorses. An unbridled freedom to touch could never be permitted.

Historically, the Library of Congress Talking Books Program refused to record books with explicit sexual content. In this way the flow of information from the sighted world to the nonsighted was strictly controlled. When sex education was introduced, it was also socialization into "acceptable" expressions of sexuality. This included only heterosexuality and only traditional gender roles. Gender and sex are regulated together by unexamined ideological structures. This is implicitly, if not explicitly, the regulation of desire, as discussed by Butler (2006) and others. Teaching this "common sense" is based so strongly in the visual world that these students are at first oblivious to gender as it is experienced and understood by the sighted. They all must study it. Gender assumes a naturalistic polarization that is exposed here as learned by many repeated lessons and performances.

I remember a story that Jesse told me. According to him, the Supreme Court had found touch to be more obscene than looking. "For example," he explained, "at the Mitchell Brothers Theater (a venue for pornography in the San Francisco Tenderloin similar to those that used to line 42nd Street in New York), patrons could watch the show, but the theater would be raided and they would be arrested if they touched any of the performers." Now here is a complicated ethical question for a feminist. Is this fair to blind men, who can only perceive through touch? After all, *Playboy* is published in Braille. Later Isabel reveals to me that she can judge breast size in women to whom she is attracted. She does this, of course, by touch, by using her lack of vision as a reason to hold on to a companion's arm as they walk along the street. This has become for her one of the multiple functions of blindness.

In this school and in all the other training programs for the blind that I have investigated, a primary goal is to teach students not to touch each other or themselves. Or, more precisely, they are taught only to touch in the ways and according to the rules of the sighted world. They are trained to be acceptable and therefore accepted in sighted society, rather than to themselves. There was never any consideration of a separate blind world. The goal was always to assimilate, to be able to pass when possible and to learn "to fake it" when they could. I had seen the results of this teaching in all the blind adults that I had met and would continue to see it in those I was yet to meet. I think that I understand them all more deeply after learning some of their lessons.

This curriculum could be named "How to Talk to Sighted People for the Blind," "How to Look Acceptable to Sighted People," "How Not to Frighten or Disgust Sighted People." It could be called "How to Pass Among Sighted People." But it is not called any of these things. It is called "Curriculum in Life Skills for the Blind" or something equally objective and neutral sounding. There are courses in maintaining eye contact and displaying appropriate facial expressions to doing gender to perceiving race. For most of them, just as for most of us who are sighted, these lessons come with all the prejudices and biases of the sighted world.

Embedded in the classes in life skills for the blind are the skills of distinction and discrimination, of dividing the human race into fragments, into categories, some of which are privileged and deemed superior to others, and into hierarchies constructed by and for those with vision. To pass successfully, a blind person must learn the theory, if not the practice, of sight, which includes the ever refined practice of discrimination, including all the "isms" practiced by the society in which they must live. As Samantha learned in formal classes how to walk and sit as a woman, how to flirt and seduce, so was Luke being given the same lessons in manhood from his peers—how to be a man, how to move in the world, and what kind of woman would serve as a trophy, a testament to his masculinity. Meanwhile Isabel was carefully studying what a lesbian looks like to a sighted lesbian. "How will a sighted person recognize me, my gendered category and sexual desires," each thought. And each figured it out in her or his own way.

But that way is not a diminished version of the sighted; it is a different way. I have made a study of appearance as it relates to first impression, and there is a large psychological literature on this topic. In my own dissertation (Kaschak 1974) I studied gendered body language of multiple family members interacting with each other and found an effect of gender and of the topic under discussion. However, that study was done by observation and ratings and lacked the depth of this work. All these years later I have carefully studied visual clues that code for gender, ethnicity, and sexual orientation (Kaschak 1993, 2010) in the United States. I cannot disagree with the minimal number of cues that these blind people used. I can only suggest that there are a plethora of cues that must hang together perceptually, that must add up to a whole in order not to confuse the cultural gaze.

Here, as elsewhere, it is the eye/brain combination that learns to recognize these arbitrary cues holistically, that weaves together the fragments and sees a whole image "right" side up, and that knows in an instant how to decipher the code. Absent sight, the performance is fragmented and reduced, just as it is carefully memorized and not well embedded in the bodies of the blind. In my own opinion, it is the meta-message that speaks the most loudly and that is use of the eyes themselves more or less boldly, flirtatiously, humbly, proudly, along with the other expressions that pass over sighted eyes and faces.

These cannot be taught seamlessly with words, and language does not fill in the blind spots as vision does, so the blind do not generally perform them well. While they signal the same emotions with the same expressions, they do so with much less frequency and in a manner that would code as subdued or overly expressive to this sighted individual. I recall Gabby mentioning this issue, saying that when she tried to be expressive to get attention she was often considered histrionic.

In their very effort to participate in gender, racialization, the blind imitate and expose it as unnatural. One more crucial question remains. What do the attempts of the blind tell us about the images and ideas of the sighted?

11

Not Seeing Is Also Believing

Why did we become blind, I don't know, perhaps one day we'll find out.

Do you want me to tell you what I think?

Yes, do.

I don't think we did go blind.

I think we are blind, Blind but seeing. Blind people who can see, but do not see.

—JOSÉ SARAMAGO

WE HAVE FINALLY ARRIVED BACK AT THE BEGINNING, the starting place of all our questions. Can we "know the place for the first time?" (Eliot 2011). I believe that we can know it much more thoroughly and deeply after our excursion. I have now borne witness repeatedly, as have all of you accompanying me, through intimate relationship with many blind people; they have all proven themselves to be avid students of a visual code of which the sighted are scarcely aware. They firmly believe in what they cannot see. They cannot see a hairstyle in combination with a face, clothing, and body language. They cannot see the subtle complexities of skin color, ethnic dress, body language, and other contextual variables. They cannot see the variety of subtle and unsubtle facial expressions that the sighted rely upon for nuanced perceptions. Their perceptions, learned from the sighted, can only remain partial and fragmented, owing more to verbal than visual limitation. The first language cannot fully translate into the second. It is no one's fault but that of the language itself.

What of the sighted who try to convey these ideas with words? I myself spent a long time in the first moments of this study trying to describe and explain color before I realized the futility of the attempts. Gender, sexuality, and race are slippery ideas. Just as they come into focus, they can collapse into multiplicity. They are meant to stand rigidly at attention and are held in that position by much that is visible and even more that remains invisible to the unquestioning eye. They haunt the sighted terrain in a ghostly fashion, seen and not seen at the same time. It is no longer the surprise that it initially was to me that they are engraved everywhere in the nonsighted zone.

It has become increasingly apparent to me that gender is what is sometimes called an informative display by ethnologists (Garfinkel 1991), more a performance than a characteristic, more mutable than fixed, more subject to cultural approval and disapproval than prior to or separate from it (Butler 1988, 2006). Of course, this performance is learned well enough to appear natural to the human eye, for which it is always rehearsing. The eye/brain duo is also complicit in creating the naturalness of a carefully developed informative display.

Race is slowly yielding to genetic decoding not as an inherent or even unitary trait, but as one that is also culturally created and defined. It is not, after all, based so much in skin color as in the symbolism of skin color. I do not mean to underestimate the literal and physical damage that has been done to individuals based on the color of skin. But these very skin colors are not what they appear to be to the cultural gaze. When we talk of black and white, we are not even seeing black and white skin, but shades of brown and a sort of pinkish yellow. It is the eye of the European explorer, conquistador, and slave trader long ago that developed this cultural gaze. It is an imperialistic gaze culturally and personally.

I have come to understand something that I did not before my time with the blind. It is racism that creates racialization and the idea of race and not the reverse. The very notion of race is born of a sense of entitlement and right to colonization and ends in an invented excuse for them. I am more convinced than ever, as are many other scholars, that race itself was invented in order to justify the acquisition and possession of slaves. Roediger (1991:20) discovered that the "term 'white' [first] arose as a designation for European explorers, traders and settlers who came into contact with Africans and the indigenous peoples of the Americas." The idea of *whiteness* next emerged in the development of America's free-labor market. White workers demanded they be entitled to a legitimate status of "freeman," a status that combined white supremacy, an exclusively occupational trade, and civil rights.

In fact, the idea of separate races can be traced to the eighteenth century when scientists undertook the classification of qualities such as intelligence, morality, or athletic ability by racial group. If one race were deemed superior, groundwork for justification of the crime of slavery was laid. Genetic variation within so-called races is actually as great as that between racial groups (Lee 1991).

Having invented it, humans began to see race until it seemed that it was really there. What are merely evolutionarily adapted differences to climate were deemed to be something much deeper and much more meaningful. They mattered in every conceivable way and eventually grew to seem natural and inevitable.

We are all complicit in this conspiracy. Our human brains permit only a complex combination of participation and resistance, even to those of us who resist as mightily as we can the racism and misogyny that enter us at every turn. We cannot patrol these borders well enough despite all the popular psychological chatter about boundaries. Psychological boundaries are elusive and imaginary. They are carved in shifting sands. Thus, when blind individuals seem to know about race, I would assert that it is actually racism that they are being taught and can repeat, invented and enforced differences in human beings.

In earlier writing (Kaschak 1993) I have suggested that the power and pervasiveness of vision and its use in evaluating and maintaining cultural rules and strategies be thought of as the workings of an indeterminate and ubiquitous observer. This observer is everywhere and nowhere at the same time. That is, any and all members of a cultural group are a part of this observation process, both looking and being seen simultaneously through the eyes of the indeterminate observer, who is no one in particular, but whose eyes shape and are shaped by what the culture sees and how it judges what it sees. These eyes see gender, race, sexual orientation, and class. In Western society of the late twentieth and early twenty-first centuries, they create and perceive separate and clear categories and pretend to discover them. They come to exist by this very act of discernment. The indeterminate observer is no one and everyone, the trickster at work. When I ventured out to study the nonsighted, I did not know yet and did not expect that this observer lives even in blind eyes. I did not yet realize that so many blind people, even absent sight, still look right into the cultural mirrors.

Vision has revealed itself to us as not just a language but a complex system of knowledge originating at the roots of the tree of knowledge and spreading throughout its branches. The universe itself is fluid and chaotic, in constant motion, but beyond human perception. We humans just cannot see most of what is all around us. None of us can see atoms, quarks, or even the electromagnetic waves in which we are bathed every moment. We are not designed to perceive any more than we need at the moment to act or to decide. We are not built to see most of what we might. It would overwhelm the senses and the mind. The visual world is much too complex; the human brain discards most of it and organizes the rest into consensually valid patterns. In an important, if not crucial, sense, we humans are designed to lie to ourselves.

Vision has revealed itself as a prior system of communication, more unconscious and perhaps less accessible than language. It is governed by its own epistemology, ways of knowing that shape every perspective and worldview. Most of us think we learn consciously and knowingly, even if this knowledge later becomes relegated to an unconscious zone. We think we see what is there, but instead we see what our senses and our own experience permit. We see and feel solid objects and separate people around us that are produced by our sensory systems. We feel our feet on solid ground with a sky above and ground below. We have to be taught that the earth moves and the sun does not, that energy precedes matter, and that all matter is formed and reformed by mattering. Seeing is not simply taking in light any more than language is stringing together words. The human brain is prepared for a grammar of vision as much as it is for a grammar of words (Chomsky and Foucault 2006).

Although nonverbal communication has typically been considered to modify language, I have come to believe that it is a prior language. The human mind learns to coordinate the two systems and not to notice that effort. Visual language is less subject to distortion and dishonesty, so that when words and facial expressions or gestures do not match, most of us rely upon the expressions and gestures. Body language affects how others see us, but it may also change how we see ourselves. Extensive research on body language reveals that we can change other people's perceptions—and even our own body chemistry—simply by changing body positions. We can change a mood by simply smiling (Scheflen 1972; Bandler and Grinder 1979). The physical is part of the context for the verbal in human eyes/mind and it is largely visual, even taking into consideration Gabby's point that a voice changes with posture.

Yet I would suggest that vision and language are not merely systems of communication, but are different epistemologies, different ways of knowing. Not having access to vision is, in a very real sense, comparable to lacking access to language. Of course, the impact on the developing mind is not as severe, but also is not as simple as having to learn visual information another way. The complexity and subtlety of the visual channels can never be fully translated. As I myself had learned through my experience with these blind people, they can only be roughly approximated in a somewhat stilted and reduced form. Samantha's sexiness and Isabel's lesbian hairstyle may be recognizable to the sighted, but are both somewhat akin to speaking with someone who is just learning your own native tongue. It is possible to communicate in simple one-syllable words, but requires effort on the part of the speaker and listener and can be fraught with minor misunderstandings and missed messages.

I think of my second language, Spanish, learned as an adult in my adopted country, Costa Rica. I speak it fluently, but do not understand many cultural nuances with the same fluency as a native speaker. For example, I am never quite sure whether to proffer a hand or a cheek when meeting someone and when to use the familiar and when the formal manner of address. This also differs among different generations and different countries. That is, I speak the language minus some unconsciously stored early context, just as a blind person may try to grasp sighted meanings.

Once when I was trying to order a taxi to the airport, I was asked my address. I launched into the kind of description that I had grown accustomed to hearing in Costa Rica. I am on the old road to Escazu across from the electric plant. The response from the other end of the telephone was quick and annoyed. "Señora, eso no es una dirección" (Ma'am, that's not an address). I had to hang up and call a native Costa Rican friend to learn that my address is instead 400 meters from the West Sabana (a park) Spoons (a soda or café). This address the taxi service understood and I was immediately able to order their service.

The human mind specializes in consolidating disconnected as well as related events or patterns and making meaning of them. This is, in fact, the primary function of the prefrontal cortex, which metabolizes memory and imagination, with the assistance of culture, into meaning. It is how each of us organizes a life so that it makes sense, so that a self emerges from raw experience, a collection of mattering maps develops. These maps of meaning are coordinated with the brain maps described by neuroscientists (Edelman 2006). Of course, these are metaphorical maps generated by the very brains under study, yet they are just as real and unreal as the ground on which we each stand, also produced by the interaction of our human senses and neurons with the raw flux of electromagnetic energy that is the "real" world (Kaschak 2013).

They are often imperceptible because as we learn them, we are taught not to be aware of them. Nonsight built right into sight, the blind spot morphs into unconscious experience. We do not know what we know and do not see what we see. These are the underpinnings of the visual system of knowing. This system of organizing knowledge is necessary, of course, or each person would be overwhelmed and perhaps paralyzed by the amount of information taken in every moment by the eyes alone. For these very reasons, learning must involve meaning. Raw experience must be organized into patterns in order to be perceived. What is banished beyond the borders of awareness becomes invisible and is the very definition of unconsciousness.

Later in the day, driving home alone in my car, I indulge my habit of listening to public radio just in time to catch the last minutes of Terry Gross interviewing Bill T. Jones, the dancer and choreographer. They are discussing performance, in particular one that won him and his late partner an award in Germany. The award was for what was called the brilliant dance presentation of the struggle between Black and White in America and secondly the homoerotic struggle. The audience saw that they were homosexuals and that one was White and one was Black. That was not at all what they had intended to depict in their dancing but, no matter how they danced, that is how they were seen.

One more question insists on giving voice to itself. It is easier to understand this compromise in the blind, but how can the sighted get away with seeing so little, living within so many intersecting vortices of attention, meaning, and desire, and trying to contain this perpetual flux in a bounded and simple vision. How much is any of us entitled to see? What is rendered invisible is rarely missed, except perhaps for the occasional stirring of an ancient longing.

Neurologists have discovered, in recent years, what they have named mirror neurons in an apparent acknowledgment of their crucial involvement in visual learning. Through the activation of this corner of the brain, every sighted person learns facial expression, gesture, and movement without the necessity of a single word being exchanged. Recently, scientists have discovered that this same mirror system can develop in humans absent sight (Ricciardi et al., 2009). In such cases the mirror system can be engaged by sound. This finding adds credence to the assertions of most of the blind people we have visited that they respond powerfully to voices.

Here is a poem that I came across in the *New Yorker* while I was writing this book. It is not about blindness of the blind, but of the sighted as age and cataracts alter visual perception in a less drastic form than complete blindness. This description is as poetic and as real as anything I have read.

MONET REFUSES THE OPERATION
Doctor, you say there are no haloes
around the streetlights in Paris
and what I see is an aberration
caused by old age, an affliction.
I tell you it has taken me all my life
to arrive at the vision of gas lamps as angels,
to soften and blur and finally banish
the edges you regret I don't see,
to learn that the line I called the horizon
does not exist and sky and water,
so long apart, are the same state of being.
Fifty-four years before I could see
Rouen cathedral is built
of parallel shafts of sun,
and now you want to restore
my youthful errors: fixed
notions of top and bottom,
the illusion of three-dimensional space,
wisteria separate
from the bridge it covers.
What can I say to convince you
the Houses of Parliament dissolve
night after night to become
the fluid dream of the Thames?

I will not return to a universe
of objects that don't know each other,
as if islands were not the lost children
of one great continent. The world
is flux, and light becomes what it touches,
becomes water, lilies on water,
becomes lilac and mauve and yellow
and white and cerulean lamps,
small fists passing sunlight
so quickly to one another
that it would take long, streaming hair
inside my brush to catch it.
To paint the speed of light!
Our weighted shapes, these verticals,
burn to mix with air
and change our bones, skin, clothes
to gases. Doctor,
if only you could see
how heaven pulls earth into its arms
and how infinitely the heart expands
to claim this world, blue vapor without end.

(Mueller 1986)

Synchronistically, I had my own cataracts removed just before completing this book. Before I could see, but not very well and only with the glasses I have worn since early childhood. Almost immediately after the surgery, I opened my eyes to a brighter and more colorful world than I had ever seen before. I saw details of people's faces and expressions more clearly than I had in years, if ever. I could not tune out the external world in a way that I had always been able to do before. I was a completely disoriented introvert. I still have not fully accommodated to my altered perception more than a year later. I find that I must do so consciously and deliberately when I awaken each day. It is too late for me to learn these visual details fluently.

In the final analysis, our eyes are set right in front of our human faces, programmed to a stationary position by ancient genes. Yet our human brains are able to invent prosthetic devices to extend that binocular vision. In fact, we are drowning in them, and they are, in turn, changing those very

brains. One day, in my neighborhood, I happened upon a robbery in progress. No one had intervened, and instead there was a small circle around
the actors, each observer with a cell phone raised filming the entire event.
I have no way of knowing whether they were thinking, "I will give this to
the police or I can't wait to post this on Facebook." Either way, vision had
replaced human action, viewing a substitute for doing. It requires little
perspicacity to notice that the sighted in many cultures are developing the
habit of looking at screens and not each other. Five people at a dinner table
next to mine in a restaurant are all looking at their devices rather than at
each other. The first time I noticed this proclivity, a few years ago, I found
it extraordinary. It has morphed into the ordinary, and I may have done it
myself once or twice. "Reality" itself is played out on the television screen,
junk food for the eyes that can binge but not purge as voyeurism metabolizes into the ordinary. Mirrors and screens substitute for "real life."

The blind want to share in our sighted illusions, in our impressions of
reality created by the alchemy of inverted images with ever evolving memory and imagination stirred in. Each of us wishes to claim our place in the
minds of others. Yet each of us lives, to a greater extent than we know,
right in the blind spot. None of us can ever see ourselves, and we must
instead depend on mirrors and reflections to try to grasp the unseen. We
must depend, as do the blind, on others' vision and others' perspectives to
get even a preliminary sense of ourselves. I asked blind people what they
would look at if they could see for twenty-four hours, but I have not asked
the sighted what they would want to see if they could look at themselves
directly. If we could see ourselves, look directly at our own faces and bodies,
look into our own eyes, we would replace all the psychotherapists in the
world—all the significant others from parents on who reflect who we are.
Yet the irony is that we can never see ourselves except in a mirror or the mirror of other people's eyes. Not one of us can ever see her whole self except
as a reflection.

Consider what our world would be like if our human eyes could look
inward as well as outward. What if we could see one hundred different colors and hues, as do pigeons and other birds, instead of the limited number
we do see? While snakes have two sets of eyes, they also have vision pits
that detect heat and see living creatures like an infrared detector (Bauchot 1994; Sekuler, Lee, and Shettleworth 1996). What if we saw a flux
of atoms instead of a relatively sturdy material world? Around us all is a

three-dimensional world that most of us take for granted, although this very dimensionality is a product of parallax, the convergence of two human eyes, in alchemical mixture with the other human senses. Our human eyes transform electromagnetic waves into colors. Other living creatures see the same environment without color, with more color, or as if fragmented by a kaleidoscope. Perhaps they do not develop visual epistemologies, but they do develop ways of seeing and knowing that introduce them to entirely different worlds from our own.

What if, looking at any person, the human eye could see all that they have been and not just a current snapshot? That very ability would change everything we know about the world and the people in it. It would approximate judging others from the inside, as we perceive ourselves, and not from the superficial exterior, the shape and colors of skin, eyes, and noses.

We humans, with our assortment of rods, cones, and blind spots, see those who people our world not only as three dimensional, but as meaningful. It is these patterns of meaning that the blind study so carefully. However, for the sighted, they need not be studied, as they are implicated in vision itself. Among the patterns seen as meaningful are dichotomous gender and sexual orientation along with racial designations loosely, if at all, based in actual color seen by the human eye. These human characteristics cannot just be a product of our eyes. They require the participation of our individual minds and cultural minds. They require context, subtext, and a lot of experience. They lie dormant until summoned and then demand to become meaningful, for mattering to be deeply embedded in matter.

I am not saying that those of us who have access to sight perceive what does not exist, but instead that we humans arrive in a universe pregnant with possibility and, from there, we have to be carefully taught what and how to see and, thus, to experience. This feedback loop fashions the neuronal connections of the brain to reinforce what has already been seen. This orchestration of the mind's eye with personal and cultural training creates each of our lives in concert.

Unlike the deaf, the blind have not developed their own language or culture. They are often isolated and scattered from each other; they speak their own careful translation of sighted language and seem to have no mother tongue, although I never did come across a nonsighted mother and child. Does this not point directly to how many of the sighted make a similar compromise between self and the many demands of sighted culture, attempting to meet or defy the complex demands of gendered and racialized meanings and the narrow acceptable possibilities of sexual expression?

I am coming to see gender and sexuality, along with racialization, more and more as a form of alchemy (Williams 1992), not solely but significantly visual, that shapes the human psyche and the human flesh. It affects the seer and the seen in equal measure. With or without light, with or without vision, illusion resides in and around us all. The blind do not have visual concepts, but have the language of visual concepts, based on hearsay and constructed from the experiences of the sighted. Only the sighted experience holistic images, which can trick the mind into thinking they see what is there.

Vision has revealed itself as an epistemology. It is the complex and fluid blend of the personal and cultural gaze. As vision proceeds to dominate cultural experience, it is crucial to the development of society and future generations, who speak visual technology fluently as those of older generations do not, that it be kept in mind as an early and pervasive epistemology. Complex codes are being mastered with every look, are a cipher in the human eye.

Residing in the parallel universe of the blind has permitted me to decipher this code in a unique way and to understand many of the connections. I look at almost everything and certainly everyone differently. For me, it has been the most exquisite kind of travel, allowing me to see with new eyes and to return home changed forever. It has transformed the ordinary and invisible into the even more ordinary and visible. I hope it has accomplished something like this for each reader who has accompanied me.

I feel morally bound to these blind people, not to the literalness of their stories, but to the best truth I can tell. I do not want to reduce their lives to rods and cones, the optical nerve or the occipital lobe. Yet none of these can be excluded either. I have tried to listen in on the conversations between biology-perception and the social-psychological milieu that shapes them and all of us. I have labored to ferret out the hidden and unconscious meanings of the psychologist, sociologist of knowledge, and ethnographer, rather than accept the surface knowledge of self-report. I have answered the question "How do we know what we know?" as deeply as I can.

Friedman (2011) has argued for defamiliarizing visual perception as a way of focusing on other forms of sensory perception, particularly the social/visual distinctions in constructions of race and gender (p. 285). She points out that "while blind people are unable to perceive certain sex differences that seem visually obvious, the sighted are equally unaware of aspects of sex that are obvious to blind people" (p. 286). I would add that the sighted are unaware of how they develop their own sighted concepts and how they change over time and through experience.

Through the imperiousness of the cultural gaze, our very eyes are colonized. Anyone can (not) see that there are an infinite array of skin colors, genders, and sexualities. Black represents an array of actual colors, as does white. How many hues are considered black or white? How many variations of gender or sexuality might there be if we simply asked? Why reduce them to a single enforced category and define those enforced memberships as natural? We, the sighted, mislead the blind just as we mislead ourselves, that there are two genders, two sexual orientations, and two or three races.

Vision comes complete with its own sort of metabolism of the extraordinary into the ordinary. We cannot maintain orientation or pay attention as we are constituted without this reduction of complexity, nor can we if we insist on seeing all the complexity around us and in us. We are like the blind person insisting she knows the difference between purple and orange. We see what we see and invent the rest.

Scientists have revealed the human brain has a fifteen-second lag that helps stabilize incoming visual information, which we don't notice bombarding us in the course of our everyday lives. Eyes tend to receive an enormous information load from dusk till dawn, and as one opens his or her eyes in the morning the brain starts its intensive work, processing incoming pictures from the surroundings, including imagery from TV screens and computer monitors. A team of vision scientists at the University of California, Berkeley and the Massachusetts Institute of Technology revealed this secret of the human brain: To save us from insanity induced by a constantly changing torrent of pictures, shapes, and colors—both virtual and real world—the brain filters out information, failing in most cases to notice small changes in a fifteen-second period of time. It actually means that what we do see is, in fact, a mixture of past and present (Goodale 2004).

The best we can do, as members of our species, is to renew our vows to see as much as possible with the vision that we do have and to remain mindful of what we do not see. Once we are shown patterns, our mind/eye tends to continue to see them. I do not invoke the popular metaphor of deconstruction, as I find it too urban and concrete. Instead I offer that

our most cherished concepts need dis-illusioning or dis-imagining periodi-
cally. The very word *spectrum* takes its meaning from the word *apparition*,
as the sighted universe is perpetually haunted by what is invisible to us as
ghosts. Just as Einstein demonstrated that time depends on clocks and the
people using them, sightless individuals have brought us to this moment,
have allowed us to see that gender(ization) and racial(ization) are products
of our own human eyes. What must be questioned are not just the qualities
that lead to these ideas becoming psychological and cultural "reality" via
the indeterminate observer, but the very force that holds them in apparently static pattern in the human eye/mind. That glue or psychological
gravity is mattering, individual and cultural, idiosyncratic and consensual.
It must be questioned.

EPISTEMOLOGY OF SIGHT

The Gaze: Masculine Perspectives

Bateson, G. 1979. *Mind and Nature, a Necessary Unity*, New York: Bantam.

Berger, J. 1972. *Ways of Seeing*. London: Penguin.

Berger, M. A. 2005. *Sight Unseen: Whiteness and American Visual Culture*. Berkeley: University of California Press.

Foucault, M. 1965 [1961]. *Madness and Civilization: A History of Insanity in the Age of Reason*. Trans. R. Howard. New York: Random House.

Foucault, M. 1973. *The Birth of the Clinic: An Archaeology of Medical Perception*. London: Tavistock.

———. 2006 [1961]. *History of Madness*. Ed. J. Khalfa. Trans. J. Murphy and J. Khalfa. London: Routledge.

Jay, M. 1993. *Downcast Eyes: The Denigration of Vision in Twentieth-Century French Thought*. Berkeley: University of California Press.

Krips, H. 2010. "The Politics of the Gaze: Foucault, Lacan and Zizek." *Culture Unbound: Journal of Current Cultural Research* 2:91–102.

Lacan, J. 1981 [1964]. "The Split Between the Eye and the Gaze." In *The Four Fundamental Concepts of Psychoanalysis*. Trans. A. Sheridan. New York: Norton.

Lacan, J., and B. Fink. 2007. *Ecrits: The First Complete Edition in English*. New York: Norton.

Merleau-Ponty, M. 1964. "Eye and mind." In *The Primacy of Perception: And Other Essays on Phenomenological Psychology, the Philosophy of Art, History, and Politics*, 159–90. Ed. J. M. Edie. Trans. C. Dallery. Evanston, IL: Northwestern University Press.

———. 1969. *The Visible and the Invisible.* Trans. A. Lingis. Evanston, IL: Northwestern University Press.

———. 1981 [1945]. *Phenomenology of Perception.* Trans. C. Smith and F. Williams.
New York: Humanities.

———. 2013 [1945]. *Phenomenology of Perception.* Trans. D. A. Landes. New York:
Routledge.

Žižek, S. 2012. *The Year of Dreaming Dangerously.* London: Verso.

The Gaze: Feminist Perspectives and Film Theory

De Lauretis, T. 1987. *Technologies of Gender: Essays on Theory, Film and Fiction.*
Self-published.

———. 2010. *Freud's Drive: Psychoanalysis, Literature and Film.* London: Palgrave
Macmillan.

Flax, J. 1993. *Disputed Subjects: Essays on Psychoanalysis, Politics, and Philosophy.*
NewYork: Routledge.

Gaines, J. 2006. "White Privilege and Looking Relations: Race and Gender in
Feminist Film Theory." In Jessica Evans and Stuart Hall, eds., *Visual Culture:
The Reader.* London: Sage.

Locher, P., R. Unger, P. Sociedad, and J. Wahl. 1993. "At First Glance: Accessibility
of the Physical Attractiveness Stereotype." *Sex Roles* 28 (11/12): 729–43.

Mulvey, L. 1975. "Visual Pleasure and Narrative Cinema." *Screen* 16 (3): 6–18.

Rabinowitz, P. 1990. "Review. Seeing Through the Gendered I: Feminist Film
Theory." *Feminist Studies* 16 (1): 151–69.

The Postcolonial or Imperial Gaze

Kaplan, E. 2004. "Global Feminisms and the State of Feminist Film Theory." *Signs*
30 (1): 1236–48.

Phenomenology of Vision and Blindness

Geyer-Ryan, Helga. 1996. "Imaginary Identity: Space, Gender, Nation." In M. Jay
and T. Brennan, eds., *Vision in Context: Historical and Contemporary Perspectives
on Sight.* New York: Routledge.

Hull, John. M. 1990. *Touching the Rock: An Experience of Blindness.* New York:
Pantheon.

Michalko, R. 2001. "Blindness Enters the Classroom." *Disability and Society* 16(3):
349–59.

Schillmeier, M. W. J. 2010. *Rethinking Disability: Bodies, Senses, and Things.* Vol. 11. Taylor and Francis.

Styre, A. 2010. *Visual Culture in Organizations: Theory and Cases.* New York: Routledge.

Developmental Issues in Vision and Blindness

Connolly, A. C., L. R. Gleitman, and S. L. Thompson-Schill. 2007. "Effect of Congenital Blindness on the Semantic Representation of Some Everyday Concepts." *Proceedings of the National Academy of Sciences* 104 (20): 8241–46.

Fraiberg, Selma. 1977. *Insights from the Blind.* New York: Basic Books.

Hirschfeld, L. A. 2008. "Children's Developing Conceptions of Race." In S. M. Quintana and C. McKown, eds., *Handbook of Race, Racism, and the Developing Child,* 37–54. Hoboken, NJ: Wiley.

Marmor, G. S. 1978. "Age of Blindness and the Development of the Semantics of Color Names." *Journal of Experimental Child Psychology* 25:267–78.

Patterson, M. M., and R. S. Bigler. 2006. "Preschool Children's Attention to Environmental Messages About Groups: Social Categorization and the Origins of Intergroup Bias." *Child Development* 77:847–60.

Roch-Levecq, A.C. 2006. "Production of Basic Emotions by Children with Congenital Blindness: Evidence for the Embodiment of Theory of Mind." *British Journal of Developmental Psychology* 24 (3): 507–28.

Perceptions of Sex, Gender, and Race in the Blind

Friedman, A. 2011. "Toward a Sociology of Perception: Sight, Sex, and Gender." *Cultural Sociology* 5 (2): 187–206.

——. 2012. "Believing Not Seeing: A Blind Phenomenology of Sexed bodies." *Symbolic Interaction* 35 (3): 284–300.

Hammer, G. 2012. "Blind Women's Appearance Management: Negotiating Normalcy Between Discipline and Pleasure." *Gender and Society* 26 (3): 406–32.

Madeline, M., and J. N. Erin, eds. 2001. *Diversity and Visual Impairment: The Influence of Race, Gender, Religion, and Ethnicity on the Individual.* New York: AFB.

Obasogie, O. K. 2010. "Do Blind People See Race? Social, Legal, and Theoretical Considerations." *Law and Society Review* 44 (3–4): 585–616.

Stienstra, D. 2002. "The Intersection of Disability and Race/Ethnicity/Official Language/Religion." Prepared for the Intersections of Diversity Seminar.

Zuckerman, M., and S. C. Kieffer. 1994. "Race Differences in Face-ism: Does Facial Prominence Imply Dominance?" *Journal of Personality and Social Psychology* 66 (1): 86–92.

QUALITATIVE RESEARCH AND METHODOLOGY

Braun, V., and V. Clarke. 2006. "Using Thematic Analysis in Psychology." *Qualitative Research in Psychology*, 3, no. 2: 77–101.

Bruner, Jerome. 1993. *Acts of Meaning: Four Lectures on Mind and Culture.* Cambridge: Harvard University Press.

Butler, J. 1988. "Performative Acts and Gender Constitution: An Essay in Phenomenology and Feminist Theory." *Theatre Journal* 40 (4): 519–31.

Camic, P. M., J. E. Rhodes, and L. Yardley, eds. 2003. *Qualitative Research in Psychology: Expanding Perspectives in Methodology and Design.* Washington, DC: APA.

David E. 2004. *Doing Research in the Real World.* London: Sage.

De Certeau, M. 1988. *The Practice of Everyday Life.* Berkeley: University of California Press.

DeVault, M. 1990. "Talking and Listening from Women's Standpoint: Feminist Strategies for Interviewing and Analysis." *Social Problems* 37 (1): 96–116.

Faugier, J. and M. Sargent. 1997. "Sampling Hard to Reach Populations." *Journal of Advanced Nursing* 26 (4): 790–97.

Fonow, M. M., & Cook, J. A. (1995). "Feminist Methodology: New Applications in the Academy and Public Policy." *Signs* 30 (4): 2211–36.

Fox-Keller, E. 1985. *Reflections on Gender and Science.* New Haven: Yale University Press.

Garfinkel, H. 1991. *Studies in Ethnomethodology.* Cambridge: Polity.

Geertz, C. 1973. "Thick Description: Toward an Interpretive Theory of Culture." In *The Interpretation of Cultures: Selected Essays*, 3–30. New York: Basic Books.

Haraway, D. 1988. "Situated Knowledges: The Science Question in Feminism and the Privilege of Partial Perspective." *Feminist Studies* 14 (3): 575–99.

Howes, D. 2003. *Sensual Relations: Engaging the Senses in Culture and Social Theory.* Ann Arbor: University of Michigan Press.

Jayaratne, T. E., and A. J. Stewart. 1991. "Quantitative and Qualitative Methods in Social Science: Current Feminist Issues and Practical Strategies." In M. Fonow and J. Cook, eds., *Beyond Methodology: Feminist Scholarship as Lived Research*, 85–106. Bloomington: Indiana University Press.

Kaschak, E. 2013a. "Contextual Assessment and Treatment of Immigrants." *Women and Therapy* 37:3, 4.

———. 2013b. "The Mattering Map: Confluence and Influence." *Psychology of Women Quarterly* 37 (4): 436–43.

Lakoff, G., and M. Johnson. 1999. *Philosophy in the Flesh: The Embodied Mind and Its Challenge to Western Thought.* New York: Basic Books.

Landman, M. 2006. "Getting Quality in Qualitative Research: A Short Introduction to Feminist Methodology and Methods." *Proceedings of the Nutrition Society* 62:429–33.

McCloskey, D. 1988. "Thick and Thin Methodologies in the History of Economic Thought." In *The Popperian Legacy in Economics*, 245–57. Cambridge: Cambridge University Press.

Mishler, E. 1986. *Research Interviewing: Context and Narrative.* Cambridge: Harvard University Press.

O'Shaughnessy, S., and N. T. Krogman. 2012. "A Revolution Reconsidered? Examining the Practice of Qualitative Research in Feminist Scholarship." *Signs: Journal of Women in Culture and Society* 37:493–510.

Paget, M. 1990. "Performing the Text." *Journal of Contemporary Ethnography* 19 (1): 136–55.

Pink, S. 2006. *The Future of Visual Anthropology: Engaging the Senses.* New York: Routledge.

Reinharz, S. 1992. *Feminist Methods in Social Research.* New York: Oxford University Press.

Scheman, N. 1988. "Missing Mothers/Desiring Daughters: Framing the Sight of Women." *Critical Inquiry* 15 (1): 62–89.

Schillmeier, M. 2006. "Othering Blindness: On Modern Epistemological Politics." *Disability and Society* 21 (5): 471–84.

Smith, D. 1987. *The Everyday World as Problematic: A Feminist Sociology.* Boston: Northeastern University Press.

Sosulski, M. R., N. T. Buchanan, and C. M. Donnell. 2010. "Life History and Narrative Analysis: Feminist Methodologies Contextualizing Black Women's Experiences with Severe Mental Illness. *Journal of Sociology and Social Welfare* 37 (3): 29–57.

Styhre, A. 2010. "Knowledge Work and Practices of Seeing: Epistemologies of the Eye, Gaze, and Professional Vision." *Culture and Organization* 16 (4): 361–76.

The Personal Narratives Group, ed. 1989. *Interpreting Women's Lives.* Bloomington: Indiana University Press.

Vannini, P., D. Waskul, and S. Gottschalk. 2011. *The Senses in Self, Society, and Culture: A Sociology of the Senses*. New York: Routledge.

Varela, F. J., E. T. Thompson, and E. Rosch. 1991. *The Embodied Mind: Cognitive Science and Human Experience*. Cambridge: MIT Press.

Weiss, Robert S. 1994. *Learning from Strangers: The Art and Method of Qualitative Interview*. New York: Simon and Schuster.

Wertz, F. J., K. Charmaz, L. M. McMullen, R. Josselson, R. Anderson, and E. McSpadden. 2011. *Five Ways of Doing Qualitative Analysis: Phenomenological Psychology, Grounded Theory, Discourse Analysis, Narrative Research, and Intuitive Inquiry*. New York: Guilford.

WORKS CITED

Amasio, D. 2008. *Descartes' Error: Emotion, Reason, and the Human Brain*. New York: Penguin.

Bailey, J. Michael, Steven Gaulin, Yvonne Agyei, and Brian A. Gladue. 1994. "Effects of Gender and Sexual Orientation on Evolutionarily Relevant Aspects of Human Mating Psychology." *Journal of Personality and Social Psychology* 66:6.

Bancroft, J. 1994. "Homosexual Orientation: The Search for a Biological Basis." *British Journal of Psychiatry* 164:437–40.

Bandler, R., and J. Grinder. 1979. *Frogs Into Princes*. Lafayette, CA: Real People.

Barrett, L. F., Wilson-Mendenhall, C. D., and L. W. Barsalou. 2014. "A Psychological Construction Account of Emotion Regulation and Dysregulation: The Role of Situated Conceptualizations." In J. J. Gross, ed., *The Handbook of Emotion Regulation*, 447–65. 2d ed. New York: Guilford.

Bauchot, R., ed. 1994. *Snakes: A Natural History*. New York: Sterling.

Beckenham. K. 1998. *How Animals See: Other Visions of Our World*. London: Croom Helm.

Bialystok, E. 2001. *Bilingualism in Development: Language, Literacy, and Cognition*. New York: Cambridge University Press.

Bird, A. 2007. "Perceptions of Epigenetics." *Nature* 447 (7143, May): 396–98.

Black, Edwin. 2001. *IBM and the Holocaust: The Strategic Alliance Between Nazi Germany and America's Most Powerful Corporation*. New York: Crown.

Bolnick, Deborah A. 2008. "Individual Ancestry Inference and the Reification of Race as a Biological Phenomenon." In Barbara A. Koenig, Sarah S. Richardson, and Sandra Soo-Jin Lee, *Revisiting Race in a Genomic Age*. New Brunswick, NJ: Rutgers University Press.

Butler, J. 1988. "Performative Acts and Gender Constitution: An Essay in Phenomenology and Feminist Theory." *Theatre Journal* 40 (4): 519–31.

———. 2006. *Gender Trouble: Feminism and the Subversion of Identity*. New York: Routledge.

Camic, P. M., J. E. Rhodes, and L. Yardley. 2003. "Naming the Stars: Integrating Qualitative Methods Into Psychological Research." In P. M. Camic, J. E. Rhodes, and L. Yardley, eds., *Qualitative Research in Psychology: Expanding Perspectives in Methodology and Design*, 3–15. Washington, DC: APA.

Castaneda, C. 1998. *The Teachings of Don Juan: A Yaqui Way of Knowledge*. Berkeley: University of California Press.

Cavalli-Sforza, L. L., P. Menozzi, and A. Piazza. 1994. *The History and Geography of Human Genes*. Princeton: Princeton University Press.

Chicago, Judy, and Edward Lucie-Smith. 1999. *Women and Art: Contested Territory.*, New York: Watson-Guptill.

Chomsky, N., and M. Foucault. 2006. *The Chomsky-Foucault Debate: On Human Nature*. New York: New Press.

Chomsky, N., and M. Ronat. 1998. *On Language*. New York: New Press.

Deepwell, Katy. 2013. "Beauty and Its Shadow: A Feminist Critique of Disinterestedness." In L. Ryan, ed., *Feminist Aesthetics and Philosophy of Art: The Power of Critical Visions and Creative Engagement*. New York: Springer.

De Lauretis, Teresa. 2010. *Freud's Drive: Psychoanalysis, Literature and Film*. London: Palgrave Macmillan.

Durgin, F. H., S. P. Tripathy, D. M. Levi. 1995. "On the Filling in of the Visual Blind Spot: Some Rules of Thumb." *Perception* 24 (7): 827–80.

Edelman, G. 2006. *Second Nature: Brain Science and Human Knowledge*. New Haven: Yale University Press.

Edelman, G., and G. Tononi. 2000. *A Universe of Consciousness How Matter Becomes Imagination*. New York: Basic Books.

Ekman, P. 1993. "Facial Expression and Emotion." *American Psychologist* 48:384–92.

———. 2012. *Emotions Revealed: Recognizing Faces and Feelings to Improve Communication and Emotional Life*. New York: Holt.

Ekman, P. and R. Davidson. 1994. *Engagement*. Ed. L. Ryan Musgrave. New York: Springer.

———, eds. *The Nature of Emotion: Fundamental Questions*, 146–49. New York: Oxford University Press.

Eliot, T. S. 2011. *Four Quartets*. In *The Collected Work of T. S. Eliot*. New York: Harcourt.

Flege, J. E., G. H. Yeni-Komshiam, and S. Liu. 1999. "Age Constraints on Second-Language Acquisition." *Journal of Memory and Language* 41 (1): 78–104.

Freeland, Cynthia. 2001. *But Is It Art? An Introduction to Art Theory*. New York: Oxford University Press.

Freud, S., J. Strachey, and P. Gay. 1952. *An Autobiographical Study*. In *The Standard Edition of the Complete Psychological Works of Sigmund Freud*. New York: Norton.

Friedman, A. 2011. "Toward a Sociology of Perception: Sight, Sex and Gender." *Cultural Sociology* 5 (2): 187–206.

———. 2012. "Believing Not Seeing: A Blind Phenomenology of Sexed Bodies." *Symbolic Interaction* 35 (3): 284–300.

Garfinkel, H. 1991. *Studies in Ethnomethodology*. Boston: Polity, 1991.

Gladstone, W. E. 1858. *Studies on Homer and the Homeric Age*. Oxford: Oxford University Press.

Glendinning, V. 1998. *Jonathan Swift: A Portrait*. New York: Harcourt-Brace.

Goodale, Melvyn A. 2004. "The Eyes Have It." *Nature Neuroscience* 7:415–15.

Gothe, J., S. A. Brandt, K. Irlbacher, S. Roricht, B. A. Sabel, and B. Ulrich-Meyer. 2010. "Changes in Visual Cortex Excitability in Blind Subjects as Demonstrated by Transcranial Magnetic Stimulation." *Brain* 125 (3): 479–90.

Griffin, C., and A. Bengry-Howell. 2008. "Ethnography." In I. A. Willig and W. Stainton-Rogers, eds., *The Sage Handbook of Qualitative Research in Psychology*, 15–31. Thousand Oaks, CA: Sage.

Hall, Edward T. 1966. *The Hidden Dimension*. New York: Anchor.

Haque F. N., Gottesman, I. I., A. H. Wong. 2009. "Not Really Identical: Epigenetic Differences in Monozygotic Twins and Implications for Twin Studies in Psychiatry." *American Journal of Medical Genetics Part C Seminars in Medical Genetics* 151C (2): 136–41.

Hein, Hilde. 2010. "Looking at Museums from a Feminist Perspective." In Amy K. Levin, ed., *Gender, Sexuality, and Museums*. London: Routledge.

———. 2011. "The Responsibility of Representation: A Feminist Perspective." In Janet Marstine, ed., *The Routledge Companion to Museum Ethics: Redefining Ethics for the Twenty-First-Century Museum*. London: Routledge.

Heisenberg, W. 1925. "Über quantentheoretische Umdeutung kinematischer und mechanischer Beziehungen." *Zeitschrift für Physik* 33 (1): 879–93.

Hill, C. E., B. J. Thompson, and E. N. Williams. 1997. "A Guide to Be Conducting Consensual Qualitative Research." *Counseling Psychologist* 25:517–72.

Hirschfeld, L. A. 2008. "Children's Developing Conceptions of Race." In S. M. Quintana & C. McKown, eds., *Handbook of Race, Racism, and the Developing Child,* 37–54. Hoboken, NJ: Wiley.

Ingles-Arkell, E. 2013. "The World That Only Formerly Blind People Can See." *Neuroscience.* Accessed April 19, 2013.

Irigary, L. 1978. "Interview." In Marie Francoise Hans and Gilles Lapouge, eds., *Les Femmes, la pornographie et l'erotisme,* 50. Paris: Seuil.

Jablonka E., and G. Raz. 2009. "Transgenerational Epigenetic Inheritance: Prevalence, Mechanisms, and Implications for the Study of Heredity and Evolution." *Quarterly Review of Biology* 84 (2): 131–76.

Johnston, E. 2009. *The Epistemology of the Gaze in Popular Discourse: A Re-Vision, The Eighteenth Century* 50 (4): 385–91.

Jordge, L. B., and S. P. Wooding. 2004. "Genetic Variation, Classification, and 'Race.'" *Nature* 36:11.

Kaschak, E. 1974. "Gender and Body Language in Families." Ph.D. diss., Ohio State University.

——. 1993. *Engendered Lives: A New Psychology of Women's Experience.* New York: Basic Books.

——. 2010. "The Mattering Map: Morphing and Multiplicity." In C. Bruns and E. Kaschak, eds., *Feminist Therapy in the Twenty-first Century.* New York: Taylor and Francis.

——. 2011. "The Mattering Map." Keynote, Pushing the Boundaries of Constructivism: Collaborating Across Theories, Applications, and Methods. Boston, July.

——. 2013. "The Mattering Map: Confluence and Influence." *Psychology of Women Quarterly* 37 (4): 436–43.

Kaschak, E., and S. Sharratt. 1988. "Gender Roles in Costa Rica: The Effect of the Presence of Males or Females." *Interamerican Journal of Psychology* 22 (1, 2): 67–74.

——. 1985. "El sexo en Latinoamerica." *Revista Nacional de la Nacion,* August, 18–22.

Katz, P. A. 2003. "Racists or Tolerant Multiculturalists: How Do They Begin?" *American Psychologist* 58 (11): 897–909.

Katz, P. A., and J. A. Kofkin. 1997. "Race, Gender, and Young Children." In S. S. Luther and J. A. Burack, eds., *Developmental Psychopathology: Perspectives on Adjustment, Risk, and Disorder,* 51–74. New York: Cambridge.

Kircher, T. T., C. Senior, M. L. Phillips, S. Rabe-Hesketh, P. J. Benson, E. T. Bullmore, M. Brammer, A. Simmons, M. S. Bartels, and A. David. 2001. "Recognizing One's Own Face." *Cognition* 78 (1): B1–B15.

"Language Acquisition." *Journal of Memory and Language.* 41:78–104.

Lavis, V. 2010. "Multiple Researcher Identities: Highlighting Tensions and Implications for Ethical Practice." *Qualitative Research in Psychology* 7:316–31.

Lee, C., and J. D. Skrentny. 2010. "Race Categorization and the Regulation of Business and Science." *Law and Society Review* 44 (3–4): 617–50.

Lee, J. D. 1991. *Ethnic Minorities and Evangelical Christian Colleges.* Lanham, MD: University Press of America.

Light, Andrew, and Jonathan Smith. 2004. *The Aesthetics of Everyday Life,* New York: Columbia University Press.

Lipton, B. 2006a. *The Biology of Belief.* New York: New Press.

———. 2006b. *The Wisdom of Your Cells: How Your Beliefs Control Your Biology.* New York: Hay House.

MacKay, I. R. A., J. E. Flege, and S. Imai. 2006. "Evaluating the Effects of Chronological Age and Sentence Duration on Degree of Perceived Foreign Accent." *Applied Psycholiguistics* 27:153–83.

Maracek, J. 2003. "Toward a Qualitative Stance in Psychology." In P. M. Camic, J. E. Rhodes, and L. Yardley, eds., *Qualitative Research in Psychology: Expanding Perspectives in Methodology and Design,* 3–15. Washington, DC: APA.

Millett-Gallant, A. 2010. *The Disabled Body in Contemporary Art.* New York: Palgrave Macmillan.

Mueller, L. 1986. *Second Language.* Baton Rouge: Louisiana State University Press.

Mustanski, B. S., M. G. Dupree, C. M. Nievergelt, S. Bockland, N. J. Schork, and D. H. Hamer. 2005. *Human Genetics* 116 (4): 272–78.

Nichter, M., and N. Vuckovic. 1994. "Agenda for an Anthropology of Pharmaceutical Rractice." *Social Science and Medicine* 39:1509–25.

Obasogie, O. K. 2010. "Do Blind People See Race? Social, Legal, and Theoretical Considerations." *Law and Society Review* 44:585–606.

Ogden, D. 2005. *The Language of the Eyes: Science, Sexuality, and Female Vision in English Literature and Culture,* 1690–927. Albany: SUNY Press.

Oleson, V. 2005. "Early Millennial Feminist Qualitative Research." In N. K. Denizen and Y. S. Lincoln, eds., Sage handbook, 235. Thousand Oaks, CA: Sage.

Omi, Michael, and Howard Winant. 1994. *Racial Formation in the United States: From the 1960s to the 1990s.* 2d ed. New York: Routledge.

Pearle, E. S. 2013. *The Reconnection: Heal Others, Heal Yourself.* New York: Hay House.

Pert. C. 1997. *Molecules of Emotion.* New York: Touchstone.

Quartz, S. R., and T. J. Sejnowski. 1997. "The Neural Basis of Cognitive Development: A Constructivist Manifesto." *Behavioral and Brain Sciences* 20:537–96.

Ricciardi, E., D. Bonino, L. Sani, T. Vecchi, M. Guazzelli, J. V. Haxby, L. Fadiga, and P. Pietrini. 2009. "Do We Really Need Vision? How Blind People 'See' the Actions of Others." *Journal of Neuroscience* 27 (31): 9719–24.

Sacks, O. 1993. "A Neurologist's Notebook: To See and Not to See." *New Yorker,* May 10.

Sagarro, J., and G. Pontiero. 1997. *Blindness.* London: Harvill.

Sandelowski, M. 1995. "Sample Size in Qualitative Research." *Research in Nursing and Health* 18:179–83.

Saramago, José. 2008. *Blindness.* Boston: Mariner.

Scheflen, A. 1972. *Body Language and the Social Order: Communication as Behavioral Control.* Upper Saddle River, NJ: Prentice-Hall.

Scheman, N. 1993. *Engenderings: Constructions of Knowledge, Authority, and Privilege.* New York: Routledge.

Sekuler, A. B., J. A. J. Lee, and S. J. Shettleworth. 1996. "Pigeons Do Not Complete Partly Occluded Figures." *Perception* 25 (9): 1109–20.

Sharratt, Sara. 2011. *Gender, Shame, and Violence.* Surrey: Ashgate.

Shilts, R. 2011. *And the Band Played On: Politics, People and the AIDS Epidemic.* New York: St. Martin's.

Simmons, R., and D. A. Blyth. 1988. *Moving Into Adolescence: The Impact of Pubertal Change and School Context.* Piscataway, NJ: Aldine Transaction.

Sykes, B. 2001. "From Blood Groups to Genes." In *The Seven Daughters of Eve,* 32–51. New York: Norton.

Unger, R. K. 2006. "Through the Looking Glass: No Wonderland Yet! (the Reciprocal Relationship Between Methodology and Models of Reality)." *Psychology of Women Quarterly* 8 (1): 9–32.

Urano, K. 2010. "Sight and Knowledge Disconnected: The Epistemology of the Visual and the Ideological Gaze in the Novels of E. M. Forster and Virginia Woolf." Ph.D. diss., Durham University.

Weihenmayer, E. 2002. *Touch the Top of the World.* New York: Basic Books.

Wells, H. G. 2011. *Complete Short Story Omnibus.* London: Gollancz.

Wertz, F. J., K. Charmaz, L. M. McMullen, R. Josselson, R. Anderson, and E. McSpadden. 2011. *Five Ways of Doing Qualitative Analysis: Phenomenological Psychology, Grounded Theory, Discourse Analysis, Narrative Research, and Intuitive Inquiry.* New York: Guilford.

Williams, P. 1992. *The Alchemy of Race and Rights: Diary of a Law Professor.* New York: Basic Books.

Wright, L. 1997. *Twins and What They Tell Us About Who We Are.* New York: Wiley.

Ziarek, Ewa Plonowska. 2012a. "Aesthetics: An Important Category of Feminist Philosophy," *Journal of Speculative Philosophy* 26 (2): 385–393.

——. 2012b. *On Feminist Aesthetics and the Politics of Modernism.* New York: Columbia University Press.

CPSIA information can be obtained
at www.ICGtesting.com
Printed in the USA
LVOW07*0810310717
543242LV00001B/4/P